DAN TOOMBS

THE CURRY GUY

Recreate over 100 of the best
British Indian Restaurant
recipes at home

Photography by Kris Kirkham

Hardie Grant

QUADRILLE

For Caroline, Katy,
Joe and Jennifer

CONTENTS

PREFACE

I started writing *The Curry Guy* blog back in October 2010. I wanted to share a few of the Indian-inspired recipes I'd developed while enjoying my passion for cooking. I'd been experimenting with Indian cookery for about 15 years so this was a way of taking it all up a notch. The thing was, I didn't want to go to all the work of writing a blog if no one read or tried my recipes. I needed a gimmick.

So it was that in March 2011, I announced to my family that I wanted to cook and eat nothing but Indian food for a whole year. Breakfast, lunch and dinner, we were going to get to know Indian food like few people outside of India did. Assuming that this was just one of my many silly ideas that I rarely followed through, my family agreed to give it a go.

I had opened a Twitter account to help promote my new venture, and shared my recipes there. In the beginning, nothing much happened. I'd write and post a recipe and no one seemed to be listening. I was enjoying teaching my kids to cook so I managed not to get too discouraged, and kept writing.

Things took a turn for the better when the *Mail Online*, the *Mirror* and the *People* heard about my quest to eat and cook only Indian food for a year, and published stories about my family and me. We were actually well into our second year by then and the stories worked. That week in 2012 my readership rocketed from hundreds to thousands.

The collection of recipes I have for you are the result of what I've learned from my visits to many outstanding chefs, and the interaction I have had with my loyal blog readers. You might wonder how a guy from Turlock, California who had never tried Indian food until he was 22 could write about British Indian restaurant (BIR) style meals and, more importantly, get them right. It was my readers who started asking me questions like why is it that the rogan josh in this or that Indian cookbook tasted nothing like the rogan josh they enjoyed at their local curry house? Why was it that chicken tikka masala or chicken korma were different from their local takeaway to when they made it at home? To be honest, I was stumped as I was experiencing the same frustrations.

Things were about to change, however. Where at one time curry-house chefs kept their secret recipes closely guarded, I soon found that they were more than happy to invite me into their kitchens in exchange for a mention on my blog and on Twitter. Many have become friends and people I know I can rely on for recipes and advice.

Whenever I could break away from the day job, I visited restaurants, learning first hand the recipes that millions of people in the UK and around the world wanted. I learned not only the recipes but many tricks of the trade.

In this cookbook you are going to learn to make many of the most popular classic British curries, tandoori dishes and sides, along with getting advice on making them perfect for your personal tastes. These recipes are the real deal! We all have that amazing curry that we must order each time we 'go out for a Ruby.' I hope this book will give you the information you need to make that dish at home.

One thing is certain. In order to get British Indian Restaurant (BIR) style food right, you are going to have to do some forward preparation. There's no way around this if you want to get it right. Once you've done the prep work though, you will be able to whip up amazing BIR curries in 10 to 15 minutes! In the time it takes to pick up your favourite Indian takeaway, you could be sitting down to a selection of delicious starters, curries, rice and naans that are even better and a lot cheaper.

Undoubtedly, there will be those who scoff at the idea of cooking a curry using a base curry sauce or adding a prepared curry powder. For decades, curry houses around the UK have prepared curries in this way, creating hugely popular dishes with the ingredients that were available to them. These curries aren't authentic Indian but they are authentic British curries, and as a nation we're crazy about them!

One more thing ... I'd love to help you with any recipe questions you may have. I'm just a tweet or Facebook chat away (@TheCurryGuy) and I'm here to help.

Happy cooking!

Dan

ABOUT THESE RECIPES

If you enjoy cooking and great British Indian restaurant (BIR) food, the fun is about to begin. In this cookbook I'm going to show you the best kept secrets for making some of the most loved curry-house style curries, tandoori and side dishes at home. What's more, after you make the essential base ingredients, you'll be able to whip up the classic British curries in just ten minutes. They will taste as good as, if not much better than those produced at your favourite Indian takeaway or restaurant. As much as I do love dining out, I've saved one heck of a lot of money and enjoyed some amazing curry feasts with friends and family at home, and you can too.

I came up with these recipes after watching them being made many times at restaurants, taking notes and photographs and, of course, through a good deal of experimentation. It's the experimentation that I found most enjoyable. Like me, you will learn not only the famous recipes but also be able to tailor them to your own tastes and dietary requirements.

With this in mind, please feel free to adjust the recipes to your own personal tastes. If you want more coconut or sugar in your chicken korma, add it. If my lamb Madras isn't spicy enough for you, add some more chilli powder or fresh chillies. If lamb vindaloo doesn't appeal to you but king prawn and mushroom vindaloo does, why not?

Remember, we're not baking cakes here. An extra teaspoon of curry powder or a little less garlic and ginger paste than called for won't ruin your curry. One exception to this is when adding chilli powder and fresh chillies. If you're not sure about the spiciness, always use less than called for. You can always add more to taste but it is difficult to cool a curry down once added.

WEIGHTS AND MEASURES

I'd like to emphasize that during my many visits to curry-house kitchens, I was rarely given exact ingredient measures for different recipes. Carefully measuring a tbsp of this or a teaspoon of that just isn't done in busy Indian restaurants. I have yet to see a curry-house chef using kitchen scales, measuring spoons or jugs. Everything is eyed up on the spot and added until the dish they are making looks, tastes and smells just right.

The only measuring tool they use is their handy chef's spoon. This is a long-handled spoon that holds 30ml, so it's the equivalent of 2 tbsp. They dip this spoon into large sauce, spice and paste containers and take out what they need. It's like watching a conductor, with the containers of spices and other ingredients all part of the symphony orchestra.

When writing these recipes, I used heaped generous tablespoon and teaspoon measures. After watching these chefs simply dip their big spoons into this or that ingredient and transferring it to the curry, it just didn't feel right to take a tbsp of a spice and then carefully flatten it off into a level tbsp. This just isn't that kind of cooking; it's much wilder.

So please use my recipes as a guideline. They are the way I make them at home, although admittedly I worked out the exact measurements for this book. After you make a few recipes, you'll soon learn how much of this or that ingredient to add to make the perfect BIR feast for you, your family and friends.

A NOTE ABOUT INGREDIENTS

Copying the recipes as I learned them was not always an option. I had to decide whether to show you the recipes as I most often saw them prepared, with commercial pastes and sauces, or go for homemade alternatives used by many chefs hoping to make their mark. I chose the latter.

When you consider how busy curry houses get at the weekends, it's no wonder many chefs choose to use commercially available pastes, spice masalas and other products. It would be a full-time job to produce homemade spice blends and pickles, which just wouldn't be economically viable for a low-cost curry house.

Personally, I enjoy experimenting with my own spice masalas and pastes and have included some of my recipes. To simply tell you to use a brand name spice paste didn't seem right for a cookbook. What I have on offer for you here are my own homemade alternatives, just as many of the chefs I've met only use their own masalas and pastes. That said, if you're in a rush or simply don't like spending a lot of time in the kitchen, the ready-made products are there for you, and from time to time I choose to use them too.

WHICH OILS?

I use cold-pressed rapeseed oil for frying. Normal vegetable oil is used most often at curry houses but I like rapeseed oil as it is one of the healthiest oils for cooking. It can be used at high temperatures and has a neutral flavour. Rapeseed oil is often confused with canola oil, which is made from rapeseed and is supposedly even better for you, so it can be substituted. In the UK rapeseed oil is often sold as vegetable oil; check ingredients on the packaging.

Ghee and mustard oil are also recommended in some recipes. Recipes just seem to taste better with ghee but I do consider it a treat and not the norm. There was a time when ghee was used a lot more in restaurant curries but these days people are more concerned about their health so it is used less often.

I love the sharp and pungent flavour of mustard oil. It has been used in Indian cookery for centuries. It has, however been banned for sale for human consumption here in the UK, and in the US, and this is stated on the labels of every brand I know. If you've ever dined out at a curry house or high-end Indian restaurant, you've probably been served dishes that were prepared with this oil.

You can of course substitute rapeseed oil but the flavour will not be the same. If using, it is best to heat it up until it begins to smoke and let it cool before heating it up again to use in your cooking.

SEASONED OIL

Seasoned oil is made and used at most good curry houses. It is the byproduct of several recipes in this book. The fried onion recipe (page 19), onion bhaji recipe (page 40) and the skimmed oil from the base curry sauce (page 22) can be used to add flavour to curries in place of plain vegetable or rapeseed oil.

HOW AND WHEN INGREDIENTS ARE ADDED

I add ingredients as I was taught, using authentic subcontinent cooking techniques to achieve optimum flavour. I want to point this out because as you begin to create your own recipes, the order in which you add ingredients is important. Oil is added first, followed by whole spices, if using. To that, chopped vegetables like onions, peppers and chillies can be added and fried before other aromatics like garlic and ginger paste go in.

Some ingredients burn faster than others, which is why they need to be added in a specific order to the hot oil. Inexpensive spices such as turmeric, chilli, cumin and coriander powder can withstand heat and cook happily from the beginning of cooking. More expensive and delicate spices such as ground cardamom seeds, nutmeg, saffron, mace, dried fenugreek (methi) leaves and homemade garam masala are best added at the end of cooking just before serving, as prolonged cooking results in them losing a lot of their flavour.

When and how you add the base curry sauce in the classic British curry recipes is also important. Just a little is added at first, which quickly begins to boil down and caramelize in the pan. There is so much flavour in the caramelized sauce and it needs to be stirred in before the rest of the base sauce and stock are added. With more liquid in the pan, this second batch can simmer away untouched unless it looks like it is burning. Some of this batch will caramelize too, which again can be scraped into the sauce for even more mouthwatering flavour.

Don't worry, all is explained in each recipe, so no need to grab your highlighter.

COOKING HEAT

In the following recipes, I suggest cooking over a medium-high heat. In most restaurants, the chef cooks over intensely high heat, much hotter than most domestic hobs can achieve. Once you get to know the recipes, you might like to try turning the heat up, but while you're practising, medium-high will be just fine. I have adjusted my recipes so that you should be able to get great results whether you are cooking on a gas or electric hob.

SERVING SIZES

When curries are prepared in curry houses, they are usually cooked in small one- to two-person portions. I have chosen to write most of my recipes to serve four. I find this better when people are getting to know how BIR cooking is done. All of the recipes can easily be halved if you wish.

INTRODUCTION TO BIR COOKING

My friend Monir Mohammed, owner of Mother India in Glasgow and author of the brilliant cookbook of the same name told me about his youth and the Glasgow curry-house scene at the time. At just 16, he was working front of house in a local curry house and a lot of the clientele were abusive and much more interested in continuing drinking and causing trouble than they were in the food.

At the time, most curry-house owners were solely interested in making money, and the staff had to simply put up with the abuse. Ingredients from the subcontinent were expensive and difficult to come by but chefs used what was available to develop dishes that would appeal to the general public. Fast service and low overheads were key to a restaurant's success. The base sauce (page 22), for example was developed over time for speed and economy.

All over the UK, Pakistani and Bangladeshi chefs entered the field not because they wanted to be chefs but to avoid having to work in factories. A chef was judged by how quickly he could cook and not by the quality of his cooking. If there was a speedy chef at one restaurant, others would try to poach him. If a restaurant was busy, others would copy their menu. Chefs and other staff would move from restaurants and take their recipes with them, which they would pass on to chefs at the new restaurant. Many found it more lucrative to set up on their own, and the cycle continued. Over the decades, the basic recipes became standardized throughout the UK. When you order a chicken tikka masala, you have a good idea of what you're going to get.

These days, it is much more important for the food to be top quality and tasty. Attention to sourcing quality ingredients and creative cooking is what makes the difference between a good and bad restaurant. The classic British recipes are similar but the ingredients are more exotic and fresher and more chefs really love what they are doing.

So the pioneers of British Indian cuisine gave us a love of Indian food. They helped create an industry worth at least £3.5 billion per year in the UK. New upmarket and expensive authentic Indian restaurants with highly trained chefs have inspired many high-street curry-house restaurateurs to offer delicious authentically cooked, quality food, while still offering the same famous curries their customers love.

I feel that great-tasting BIR food is 90% down to the products you put into it and 10% down to how it is cooked. I'm going to show you how to cook these famous recipes. All you need to do now is follow a few simple rules and you're in for a treat.

RULE #1
Only use the freshest ingredients you can get your hands on. Even the best chefs in the world can't do much with stale spices and poor-quality meat and vegetables. We are so lucky to have excellent farmers' markets, butchers, fishmongers and spice suppliers here in the UK. Use them.

RULE #2
Take an afternoon to make the base ingredients. Out of all of these recipes, only the base curry sauce (page 22) needs to be made from scratch to get that awesome texture, aroma and flavour that is the BIR curry. Others like garlic and ginger paste and the spice blends can be purchased commercially. Remember, though: fresh is best and you will notice a difference in the end result.

RULE #3
Add the ingredients in the order I've specified.

RULE #4
Have fun! Choose a time to cook when you really feel like cooking. You'll enjoy it much more.

RULE #5
Other than rules one through four, there are no rules. Along with the recipes, I included many alternative ideas for making them your own. Just go for it! If it sounds good, it probably is.

EQUIPMENT AND PRESENTATION

No special 'Indian' cooking equipment is needed to prepare these recipes. You will probably already have everything you require to cook. This is a list of useful utensils, pots and pans that will come in handy both for cooking and presentation:

★ 6-litre (6 US quart) heavy-based saucepan with tight-fitting lid
★ 3-litre (3 US quart) heavy-based saucepan with tight-fitting lid
★ Food processor
★ Spice grinder or pestle and mortar
★ Blender (jug or hand-held)
★ Large stainless-steel frying pan
★ Large wok
★ Large roasting tray with a wire rack
★ Pressure cooker
★ Large mixing bowls
★ Wire mesh spoon
★ 30ml (1 oz) volume long-handled chef's spoon
★ Good-quality chef's knife – please don't go for one of those inexpensive knife sets! If you're on a budget, get one good-quality chef's knife and you'll have everything you need
★ Measuring jug
★ Barbecue with flat skewers – the skewers are optional as you can always cook on the grill, but skewers add a lot to the presentation
★ Spice dabba – this is a large, airtight container that holds several smaller containers for storing spices. They are designed for the home cook and wouldn't be used at most restaurants. Any airtight containers will do for storing spices
★ Balti pans, karahis and/or handis – these are totally optional but do add a lot to the presentation of your meal. They can be picked up quite inexpensively at Asian shops and online. More on that in the balti, karahi and handi recipe section (see pages 81–85).

YOUR INGREDIENT MISSION CONTROL PANEL

Every BIR chef has their most important spices, pastes and sauces within easy reach so that they can dip their chef's spoon into them and take out what they need as they cook. To watch a professional chef do this is quite impressive. Often they are cooking many different curries at once. With some practice, you will be able to do this too.

You will use a lot of different ingredients in the following recipes. I have included a list in the ingredients section on page 154. Some ingredients, however, are used more often than others.

Here's a list of ingredients that most chefs have in close proximity:

★ Mixed powder (see page 17)
★ Garam masala (see page 14)
★ Tandoori masala (see page 15)
★ Garlic and ginger paste (see page 18)
★ Chilli powder
★ Ground cumin
★ Ground coriander
★ Ground turmeric
★ Dried fenugreek (methi) leaves
★ Coconut flour
★ Ground almonds
★ Spice pastes (depending on chef)
★ Sugar
★ Salt*

*A good dose of salt helps bring out the flavours of the spices. Many people are reducing their salt intake these days, but a generous sprinkling of the stuff is needed to brighten up any curry. The amount you use is a personal thing so I haven't included exact measurements in most recipes. Even when used liberally, your homemade curries will probably have one heck of a lot less salt and taste much better than those ready meals found at the supermarket.

BASE
RECIPES

WHEN TRYING A RECIPE, FIRST LOOK TO SEE WHICH BASE RECIPES YOU NEED TO MAKE.

Out of all the base recipes I've included in this section, only the base curry sauce must be homemade to produce that instantly recognizable BIR-style curry. Everything else is commercially available. Even the mixed powder can be produced using ready-made masalas and spice powders. So you can take shortcuts if you want or you could make them much better.

Making delicious curry-house food is all about building layer upon layer of mouthwatering flavour. Only the best curry houses, like those I've featured, prepare everything fresh. This is especially so with spice masalas and pastes that can be expensive and time-consuming to prepare for a packed restaurant. You probably won't be cooking for that many people, so use it to your advantage and make those awesome layers of flavour go to work for you.

Even pre-cooking your meat, poultry and vegetables can add a lot of excitement to a dish. You could of course cook these from raw but it will take longer and you'll be missing out on one or more of the things that can make British Indian restaurant cuisine so amazing. These are time-saving preparations that not only make cooking faster but really please the palate.

SPICE BLENDS (MASALAS)

It's best to purchase whole spices and then roast and grind them as required. Once the spices have been roasted and ground, they lose their aroma and flavour quickly. If I didn't have to work for a living, I'd definitely do this whenever I cooked Indian food, but I do, so I don't. I cook a lot of curries every week so it makes much more sense to prepare my spice masalas in larger batches.

I find roasting and grinding my own spice masalas quite therapeutic. In fact, I usually make them after a busy day at work or on Sundays when I'm trying to take my mind off Monday.

These blends can be roasted and ground in minutes, and they can be stored in airtight containers in a cool, dark location such as a cupboard for up to two months without losing much flavour. That spectacular aroma you get from freshly ground spices will mellow substantially faster though. When single ground ingredients are called for such as ground cumin and ground coriander, it is always best to roast the whole seeds first as described in the following recipes. I always have home roasted and ground cumin and coriander on hand.

SPICE PASTES

Another way to store large batches of spice masalas is to make them into a paste. To do this, mix your masala in a pan with enough water to form a thick paste. Add about 125ml (½ cup) rapeseed oil and fry over a medium-high heat for about 30–60 seconds. Be extra careful not to burn the spices, and stir continuously. Store in an airtight, sterilized (see page 139) glass jar in a cool, dark location like a cupboard or the fridge.

You can make a paste out of any spice masala recipes in this book. These pastes can be added to curries and marinades in the same way you add dry spice masalas.

If you're interested in making your own spice masalas and pastes, I recommend getting a good spice grinder. I use a Waring spice grinder that is available online. With it, you can achieve very fine powders. I've been using mine for years. You could also find less expensive grinders that will do a good job.

GARAM MASALA

MAKES 170G, 18 TBSP, 1½ CUPS

Garam masala is a blend of warming, aromatic spices. In India, the ingredients used can vary greatly from region to region and even from family to family, and most home and professional chefs will have their own special recipe. This is one of mine, and in it I use the same spices that are popular in northern India, Bangladesh and Pakistan, essential for achieving that curry-house flavour.

Garam masala plays an important part of the mixed powder (see p17) used in most of the BIR curries in this cookbook, and is also added on its own to a lot of recipes. Sprinkling it over your finished curries is a good way to add a touch more excitement to the dish.

6 tbsp coriander seeds
6 tbsp cumin seeds
5 tsp black peppercorns
4 tbsp fennel seeds
3 tsp cloves
7.5cm (3in) piece of cinnamon stick or cassia bark
5 dried Indian bay leaves (cassia leaves)
20 green cardamom pods, lightly bruised
2 large pieces of mace

Roast all the spices in a dry frying pan over a medium-high heat until warm to the touch and fragrant, moving them around in the pan as they roast and being careful not to burn them. If they begin to smoke, take them off the heat.

Tip the warm spices onto a plate and leave to cool, then grind to a fine powder in a spice grinder or pestle and mortar.

Store in an airtight container in a cool, dark place and use within 2 months for optimal flavour.

CHAAT MASALA

MAKES 160G, 12 GENEROUS TBSP, SCANT 1¼ CUPS

Chaat masala, which has a quite distinctive flavour, is usually used in small amounts, sprinkled over finished dishes and included in marinades to give them a bit more kick. Citric acid is used in a lot of commercial brands but I've chosen to use the more authentic and healthier amchoor (dried mango powder), which gives the spice blend a nice citric flavour.

Another important ingredient is the black powdered salt. I've only seen this in Asian grocers and a few gourmet spice shops. It has a strong sulphur aroma that may take some getting used to, but before long you'll probably be hooked.

3 tbsp cumin seeds
3 tbsp coriander seeds
1 tsp chilli powder
4 tbsp amchoor (dried mango powder)
3 tbsp powdered black salt
1 tbsp freshly ground black pepper
Pinch of asafoetida powder
1 tbsp dried mint (optional)
1 tbsp garlic powder
1 tsp ajwain (carom) seeds

Roast the cumin and coriander seeds in a dry frying pan over a medium heat until warm to the touch and fragrant, moving them around in the pan as they roast and being careful not to burn them. If they begin to smoke, take them off the heat. Tip onto a plate to cool.

Grind the roasted seeds to a fine powder in a spice grinder or pestle and mortar. Add the remaining ingredients and grind some more until you have a very fine powder.

Store in an airtight container in a cool, dark place and use as needed, within 2 months for optimal flavour.

TANDOORI MASALA

MAKES 120G, 13 GENEROUS TBSP,
1¼ CUPS

Most commercial tandoori masalas taste
fantastic because they are loaded with salt and
tangy citric acid powder. The spices used are
usually quite cheap, like ground coriander
and cumin, and they are made more visually
appealing with the use of red food colouring.

I use a lot more spices and leave the salt
and citric acid powder out. You can always add
more salt to the finished dish which gives you a
lot more control over the end result. I substitute
the natural tanginess of amchoor powder for
the citric acid powder. If you would like to add
red food colouring, remember that your masala
will not be the bright red of commercial brands.
Food colouring powder becomes redder when
it is stirred into a sauce.

3 tbsp coriander seeds
3 tbsp cumin seeds
1 tbsp black mustard seeds
5cm (2in) piece of cinnamon stick or cassia bark
Small piece of mace
3 dried Indian bay leaves (cassia leaves)
1 tbsp ground ginger
2 tbsp finely ground garlic powder
2 tbsp dried onion powder
2 tbsp amchoor (dried mango powder)
1 tbsp (or more) red food colouring powder (optional)

Roast the whole spices in a dry frying pan over
a medium-high heat until warm to the touch
and fragrant, moving them around in the pan
as they roast and being careful not to burn them.
If they begin to smoke, take them off the heat.
Tip onto a plate to cool.

Grind to a fine powder in a spice grinder
or pestle and mortar and tip into a bowl. Stir
in the ground ginger, garlic powder, onion
powder and amchoor.

Stir in the red food colouring powder
(if using). The masala will not look overly
red like the commercial brands. Store in an
airtight container in a cool, dark place and use
as required, within 2 months for optimal flavour.

TANDOORI MASALA PASTE

I always like to have a little tandoor masala paste
and Kashmiri paste on hand. As the spice masalas
are first roasted and then fried, the resulting
pastes can be added at the end of cooking to
give your curries a nice flavour boost when
desired. Following is my Kashmiri paste recipe.
You can make a tandoori masala paste using
the previous tandoori masala recipe. Just
follow the frying instructions for Kashmiri
paste below. Both pastes can be stored in
airtight containers in the fridge for about
two months with little loss of flavour.

KASHMIRI PASTE

MAKES 1 JAR

4 tbsp coriander seeds
2 tbsp fennel seeds
4 tbsp cumin seeds
1 tbsp black peppercorns
2 tbsp fenugreek seeds
3cm piece of cinnamon stick or cassia bark
10 Kashmiri dried red chillies, or to taste
3 Indian bay leaves (cassia leaves)
½ tsp ground turmeric
125ml (½ cup) rapeseed oil, plus more if needed
100ml (scant ½ cup) white wine vinegar

Heat a dry frying pan over a medium-high heat.
Add the whole spices, dried chillies and Indian
bay leaves and roast until warm to the touch and
fragrant. Remove the spices from the heat if they
begin to smoke. Tip onto a plate to cool, then
grind to a very fine powder in a spice grinder
or using a pestle and mortar.

Return the ground spices to the frying pan,
and add the turmeric and just enough water to
make a thick paste. Add the oil to the pan and
place over a medium-high heat.

Stir continuously until the spices begin to
sizzle a bit and the oil rises to the top, 30 seconds
to 1 minute. Take off the heat, add the vinegar
and stir well. Spoon into a sterilized jar (see p139)
with an airtight lid. This will keep in the fridge
for at least 2 months. Use as required.

MADRAS CURRY POWDER

MAKES 285G, 27 GENEROUS TBSP, 2½ CUPS

Commercially prepared curry powders date back to the 18th century, when spice blends were prepared by Indian merchants to sell to British army and government officials returning to Britain during the British Raj. It was a way of taking the flavours of India home with them.

Unlike garam masalas, which are blends of warming spices, curry powders usually contain other complementary ingredients, with chillies often added to produce spicier blends. This version is spicy but not overly so. If you or the people you will be cooking for don't like spicy food, you can leave the dried chillies and chilli powder out.

6 tbsp coriander seeds
6 tbsp cumin seeds
4 tbsp black peppercorns
2 tbsp fennel seeds
2 tbsp black mustard seeds
12cm (4½ in) piece of cinnamon stick or cassia bark
4 Indian bay leaves (cassia leaves)
3 tbsp fenugreek seeds
3 star anise
15 cardamom pods, lightly bruised
8 Kashmiri dried red chillies (optional)
2 tbsp ground turmeric
2 tbsp hot chilli powder (optional)
1 tsp garlic powder
2 tsp onion powder

Roast all the whole spices, including the dried chillies, if using, in a dry frying pan over a medium-high heat until warm to the touch and fragrant, moving them around in the pan as they roast and being careful not to burn them. If they begin to smoke, take them off the heat.

Tip the warm spices onto a plate and leave to cool, then grind to a fine powder in a spice grinder or pestle and mortar. Add the turmeric, chilli powder, if using, garlic powder and onion powder, and stir to combine.

Store in an airtight container in a cool, dark place and use within 2 months for optimal flavour.

PANCH PORAN (INDIAN FIVE SPICE)

This whole spice blend is available in Asian spice shops already mixed, so you don't actually need to make your own. Panch poran does vary from region to region in the subcontinent but this is the most common blend in UK curry houses.

Some cooks prefer to use less fenugreek as the seeds can be quite bitter. You'll have to experiment with that one.

Equal amounts of:
Cumin seeds
Fenugreek seeds
Brown mustard seeds
Fennel seeds
Nigella seeds (black onion seeds)

For best results, roast the spices in a dry frying pan over a medium-high heat until fragrant. I usually roast them just before using.

CUMIN & CORIANDER POWDER

I am a collector of Indian cookbooks and read and cook from them often. One thing I've noticed over the years is that in authentic Indian cookery, cumin and coriander powders are usually added in equal measures. I find it so convenient to have this simple roasted spice blend on hand.

Equal amounts of:
Cumin seeds
Coriander seeds

Roast in a dry frying pan until warm to the touch and fragrant. Let cool and then grind into a fine powder. Store in an airtight container for up to 2 months.

MIXED POWDER

MAKES 17 GENEROUS TBSP

I have to emphasize how important this recipe is. It's one of the secret ingredients that makes BIR curries what they are. You will use it in almost all of the classic curries in this book.

The flavours of cumin, coriander, paprika and turmeric are in most BIR curries, and mixed powder makes it possible to add these spices all in one go, along with curry powder and garam masala. Obviously, you can adjust the flavour of your curry by adding a little more of the individual spices or masalas to taste, but adding mixed powder is usually enough to get the task of seasoning off to a good and easy start.

When I first began experimenting with BIR recipes, and before I knew of the existence of this widely used spice blend, I would add the spices individually, which works fine, but slows down the cooking process.

I have to say it wasn't easy to get the recipe because no one – and I mean no one – was giving it away. They would wave me off and say that it was just 'mixed powder'. It looked like garam masala or curry powder and I wrongly assumed that was what it was. When I finally saw it being made by chance at my local restaurant, I didn't pay attention to anything else in the kitchen. It all seemed so obvious, but it wasn't until that afternoon.

I drove home and heated up some base curry sauce while I combined the ingredients for the mixed powder recipe from memory.

With that one secret blend, my BIR curries suddenly became much less complicated to make. I finally had what I didn't even realize I was looking for!

I've since learned that many chefs also add a little ground fenugreek to their mixed powder, but as it is quite strong and bitter I only add as required to some curries at the cooking stage. There is, after all, already a little fenugreek in the mix from the curry powder used.

Since I learned this recipe, you wouldn't believe how many chefs have challenged me, asking if I knew what was in their special blend. They're amazed when I name the ingredients exactly. This one is no longer a secret.

As with the garam masala and curry powder recipes (see pages 14 and 16), it is a good idea to roast whole cumin and coriander seeds then grind them to a powder for that extra flavour boost. If you only want to make a little or you want to make a lot more, simply substitute the word 'tbsp' with 'parts'.

3 tbsp ground cumin
3 tbsp ground coriander
4 tbsp curry powder
3 tbsp paprika
3 tbsp ground turmeric
1 tbsp garam masala (see p14)

Mix all the ingredients together, store in an airtight container in a cool, dark place, and use as needed. If you are using fresh, homemade garam masala and curry powder in your blend, your mixed powder should last for up to 2 months without losing much flavour.

PREPARED SAUCES, STOCKS AND PASTES

This is where the real magic begins! It's time to make some more of the base ingredients that will get people talking about your Indian food, far and wide.

SPICE STOCK

MAKES SCANT 1 LITRE (4 CUPS)

I usually make a batch of spice stock at the same time I make the base curry sauce. This isn't one you really need to watch closely while cooking so it's a good way of getting two jobs done at once. The aromatic strained stock can be added to curries when a little more liquid is desired to thin the sauce. So could water, for that matter, but this stock does give curries more depth.

Handful of green cardamom pods, lightly bruised
15 Indian bay leaves (cassia leaves)
2.5cm (1 in) piece of cinnamon stick or cassia bark
20 black peppercorns
Large handful of star anise
1 tsp roasted cumin seeds (see p12)
Large bunch of coriander (cilantro), stems and leaves roughly chopped
1 or more fresh green chillies, to taste, halved lengthways (optional)

Put 1 litre (4¼ cups) of water in a pan and bring to a rolling boil. Throw in the herbs and spices and stir to combine. Reduce to a simmer and cook for about 30 minutes. Strain through a fine sieve and use immediately or store in airtight plastic containers in the fridge for up to 3 days. It also freezes well.

GARLIC AND GINGER PASTE

MAKES 15 GENEROUS TBSP

Garlic and ginger paste is used in almost every curry. It's so easy to make and tastes far better than any commercially available alternative. If you would like a little more control over the amount of garlic and ginger that go into your creations, make a separate garlic paste and/or a ginger paste in the same way.

150g (5½ oz) garlic, chopped
150g (5½ oz) ginger, peeled and chopped

Place the garlic and ginger in a food processor or pestle and mortar and blend with just enough water to make a smooth paste. Some chefs finely chop their garlic and ginger instead, which is a good alternative to making a paste. Store in an airtight container in the fridge for up to 3 days and use as needed. If you're planning a curry party, go ahead and get this job ticked off early.

I often make larger batches of pastes and freeze them in ice cube trays. Frozen cubes can be transferred to airtight plastic bags in the freezer, ready for when you get that curry craving. Be sure to let them defrost a little first.

GREEN CHILLI PASTE

Whenever green chillies are called for in a recipe, you could use an equal amount of this paste. Any fresh green chillies will do. Generally speaking, the larger the chilli, the milder it is.

I usually use green chillies like bird's eye or bullet chillies

Simply blend the amount you require with just enough water to make a paste and use as required. The chilli paste can be frozen in ice cube trays just like garlic and ginger paste.

TOMATO PURÉE

This is simply a thin purée of tomatoes used in many curries for flavour and colour. Here are two ways you can make it.

METHOD 1

Mix 1 part concentrated tomato paste with 3 parts water.

METHOD 2

Blend a 400g tin (2 cups) of plum tomatoes to a smooth purée. Add a little concentrated tomato paste if you want a deeper red colour.

NOTE: You could also use sieved, unseasoned Italian passata.

RAW CASHEW PASTE

Raw cashew paste is used in curries – both authentic and BIR – to thicken the sauce and to add flavour.

It is most commonly used in BIR chicken korma and lamb rogan josh but you could really add it to any curry. Why not? It's good.

Soak raw cashews (quantity as needed) in cold water for about 30 minutes. Drain and place the cashews in a spice grinder or blender. Add just enough fresh water to blend to a paste. That's it. You're done.

Transfer to a bowl and store in the fridge for up to 3 days.

FRIED ONIONS AND ONION PASTE

RECIPE CAN BE ADJUSTED FOR YOUR REQUIREMENTS

It's no secret that fried onions taste amazing. They are an essential ingredient for dopiaza curries and biryanis and also work well in marinades. You can even blend the onions with a little water or to form a paste that can be added to almost any curry to make them a little more interesting.

Don't throw the cooking oil out. Use it in your curries instead of plain oil – remember those layers of flavour I was talking about? Well this onion-infused cooking oil is a good one.

Rapeseed oil, for deep-frying
2 large onions, finely sliced

Heat enough oil for deep-frying in a large, heavy-based pan over a high heat. Test to see if it is hot enough by dropping a piece of onion in the oil; if it sizzles immediately and floats to the top, the oil is ready. Add the sliced onions and fry until they turn light brown, about 5 minutes. They will continue to cook once out of the oil so be sure to get them out when they are still light brown in colour.

Using a wire mesh spoon, remove the fried onions to a plate lined with kitchen paper, to soak up the excess fat. Store in a cool, dry place in an airtight container until ready to use. These will keep for up to a week.

THE COMMON MISCONCEPTION ABOUT THE BASE CURRY SAUCE

From Spanish sofrito to Creole holy trinity, almost every cuisine has dishes that begin with a humble mixture of aromatic ingredients. These are the first ingredients to hit the pan, fried in a little fat before the star ingredients like seafood, vegetables or meat are added. In authentic Indian cookery, this is called a base masala, and usually consists of frying finely chopped onions, garlic and ginger paste, chillies, diced tomatoes and a medley of whole or ground warming spices.

Many connoisseurs of authentic Indian food have criticized the one-sauce-fits-all base curry sauce used at curry houses, but personally I feel this is unfair. In most restaurants, this aromatic base sauce is cooked fresh daily. Without it, you would have to wait much longer for your curries when you dine out. It would also mean more last-minute work in front of the stove, and higher prices, as the base sauce makes it possible for chefs to cook, plate and serve many different curries quickly and easily. Visit the kitchen of a busy curry house or Indian takeaway and you are almost certain to see a large saucepan of curry sauce simmering away on the stove, used as a base for most, if not all, of the restaurant's curries. Although they are usually quite similar, each restaurant has their own special recipe.

Many people have been wrongly led to believe that using the same sauce for all curries makes them taste the same. Perhaps in bad restaurants this is true but not in the best curry houses. The base sauce may be basic but there is so much you can do with it to give each curry its own unique flavour and texture.

The base sauce is essentially what is referred to as a daag in northern India and Pakistan. It is common to see housewives and domestic servants prepare a cooked masala (daag) so that they can conveniently prepare a meal quickly and easily. Daags, like the base curry sauce, can be made in large batches and frozen.

This smooth curry sauce 'gravy', more than any other ingredient, is what gives British Indian restaurant (BIR) style curries their distinctive flavour and texture. If you have a six-litre (six US quart) stockpot, it's the perfect size for this large batch recipe.

I like to describe the base curry sauce as a slow-cooked onion and vegetable stock. It doesn't have a lot of flavour, although it does taste good. Rarely are chillies or chilli powder added, as the base sauce needs to be used in everything from the mildest korma to the spiciest vindaloo. The finished sauce needs to be runny like a Sunday dinner gravy or full-fat milk; it will cook down and thicken quickly as each curry is prepared over high heat.

BASE CURRY SAUCE (LARGE BATCH)
MAKES 6 LITRES (6 QUARTS) OR ENOUGH FOR 22–24 SERVINGS

2kg (4½ lb) (about 15) Spanish onions, roughly chopped
1 tsp salt
225g (½ lb) carrots, peeled and chopped
120g (4¼ oz) cabbage, chopped
100g (3½ oz) red pepper (bell pepper), deseeded and diced
100g (3½ oz) green pepper (bell pepper), deseeded and diced
1 x 400g tin (2 cups) chopped tomatoes
9 tbsp garlic and ginger paste (see p18)
750ml (3 cups) rapeseed oil
3 tbsp garam masala (see p14)
3 tbsp ground cumin
3 tbsp ground coriander
3 tbsp paprika
2 tbsp ground fenugreek
1 tbsp ground turmeric

Place the onions in a large 6-litre (6 US quart) stockpot and top with the rest of the vegetables, tomatoes and garlic and ginger paste. Pour in the oil and about a litre (1 US quart) of water. Stir to coat and place the pot over medium high heat. Bring to a simmer and then reduce to the heat to low and simmer gently, covered for about 45 minutes.

Now add another 2 litres (2 US quart) water and stir in the spices. Continue simmering for another 30 minutes. When the oil rises to the top and your veggies are soft, you're ready to blend. Carefully skim the seasoned oil off the top for use in your curries. It keeps indefinitely in an airtight container.

Using a hand-held blender, blend for about 4 minutes until the sauce is super smooth, with no chunks and not at all grainy. This step can be done in a blender in batches, but it takes a lot more time.

You will notice that the blended sauce, about 3 litres (3 US quarts), is quite thick, perfect for storing in the fridge or freezing. When you use it in your curries, you will need to double the volume with water, or until it is about the same thickness as full-fat milk.

Use immediately or store in the fridge for up to 3 days or freeze in 750ml (3 cup) portions for up to 3 months.

NOTE: The finished sauce 'gravy' is thin, just like those used at most restaurants. If your hob is not able to achieve really high heats, you might find that it is taking too long to reduce when cooking your curries. You can always add less water to your next batch if you find this to be the case, or reduce it before adding.

To make a small batch of base sauce, you can simply halve the recipe on page 22. That said, I recommend making the large batch as it keeps in the fridge for 3 days and can be frozen for up to three months. When making a small batch of sauce, I find using a pressure cooker really speeds up the process without jeopardising flavour. If you have one, you can make this small batch often as it takes only minutes to prepare, which makes more sense than spending a long time making a small amount. Any pressure cooker will do the job but I like to use a countertop one and set it to stew. Oil that rises to the top during cooking can be skimmed off and used instead of plain oil in your curries for more flavour.

BASE CURRY SAUCE (SMALL BATCH)
MAKES ENOUGH FOR ABOUT 8–10 SERVINGS

150ml (5 tbsp) rapeseed oil
800g (1¾ lb) Spanish onions, roughly chopped
25g (1 oz) carrot, peeled and chopped
25g (1 oz) cabbage, chopped
40g (1½ oz) red pepper (bell pepper), deseeded and diced
40g (1½ oz) green pepper (bell pepper), deseeded and diced
150g (5½ oz) tomatoes, diced
3 tbsp garlic and ginger paste (see p18)
1½ tsp ground cumin
1½ tsp ground coriander
1½ tsp ground fenugreek
1½ tsp paprika
1½ tsp ground turmeric
1½ tsp garam masala (see p14)

Heat the oil in the pressure cooker pan. When hot, add the onions and fry for about 5 minutes until soft and translucent but not browned. Add the remaining ingredients and stir it all to combine. Fry for a further minute or so.

Pour in 750ml (3¼ cups) water and secure the pressure cooker lid. Cook on high pressure for 10 minutes then carefully open the pressure valve to release the steam. If using a countertop pressure cooker, set to stew.

When your pressure cooker lid is ready to remove, it's time to blend your sauce. Skim off any seasoned oil floating at the top for use in later curries. Blend the sauce until it is very smooth. About four minutes should do. The sauce will be quite thick, perfect for freezing. When you use it in your curries, you will need to thin it with water or stock until it has the same consistency as full fat milk. Usually doubling the volume should make it perfect for use.

TIP: With this and the large batch sauce, you might like to experiment with different flavours. Try substituting the cooking stock from pre-cooked chicken or meat (pages 26 and 27) for the water.

PRE-COOKED MEAT, POULTRY, PANEER AND VEGETABLES

Following is a selection of pre-cooked ingredients that you can use in your curries just like they do at UK curry houses. This not only saves time at restaurants but also adds flavour. The pre-cooked stewed chicken and meat recipes as well as the fried paneer and vegetables can all be added to the classic British curry sauces as you like.

Also hugely popular are barbecued meats, paneer and vegetables. Chicken tikka masala, for example just wouldn't be the same without those nicely charred pieces of chicken (see page 92), whereas stewed chicken, in my opinion is a better bet for a curry like chicken dhansak. That said, these curries are all yours, so use whatever pre-cooked ingredient you like.

Unlike curries in the subcontinent where meat is usually cooked on the bone, British curries are made with bite-sized pieces of boneless meat.

Pre-cooking the chicken until it is just cooked through not only makes cooking in most Indian restaurants faster, but tastier too.

The cooking stock can be added to chicken curries and gives a fantastic flavour. Simply remove the chicken pieces from the liquid and then strain it. You could also throw in a chicken carcass or two while cooking the chicken. Remove the chicken pieces (tikka) when cooked but let the sauce simmer, adding a little water if necessary until you have a beautiful, rich stock. When time permits, I let mine simmer for a couple of hours. It tastes amazing. When your stock is ready, strain it and use it to thin curry sauces when necessary or simply to give the curry more depth of flavour.

Both the chicken and the stock can be stored in the fridge for up to 3 days. They can also be frozen for up to 2 months without much loss of flavour. Always defrost both and heat the stock before using.

PRE-COOKED STEWED CHICKEN
MAKES ENOUGH FOR ABOUT 10 SERVINGS

4 tbsp rapeseed oil
5 green cardamom pods, lightly bruised
10 black peppercorns
2.5cm (1 in) piece of cinnamon stick or cassia bark
1 tsp cumin seeds
1 tsp coriander seeds
3 Indian bay leaves (cassia leaves)
2 large onions, finely chopped
½ tsp sea salt
2 tbsp garlic and ginger paste (see p18)
1 tsp ground turmeric
2 x 400g tins (4 cups) chopped tomatoes
2kg (4½ lb) skinless, boneless chicken thighs or breasts, cut into bite-sized pieces (tikka)
Spice stock (see p18) or water
1 tsp garam masala (see p14)

NOTE: Chicken breast meat is used at most curry houses because it has a nice texture and looks good too. Chicken thigh meat isn't as pretty but has a lot more flavour.

Heat the oil in a pan over a medium-high heat until small bubbles form. Add the whole spices and bay leaves, and stir continuously for about 30 seconds, to release their flavours into the oil.

Add the onions and stir regularly for about 10 minutes until soft and translucent. Sprinkle the salt over the top; this will help release moisture from the onions.

Now spoon in the garlic and ginger paste, followed by the turmeric; the pan will sizzle as the paste releases its moisture. When your kitchen becomes fragrant with the magnificent aroma of garlic and ginger, tip in the tomatoes. Reduce the heat to medium and let the ingredients simmer and get to know each other for about 5 minutes. Add the chicken pieces and just enough spice stock or water to cover the chicken.

Reduce the heat and let the stock softly bubble until the chicken is just cooked through; don't overcook it. Stir in the garam masala and, using a slotted spoon, remove the chicken pieces for use in your curries, reserving the cooking stock. A little of this added to your chicken curries makes them even more delicious.

TIP: If freezer space is an issue but you want to have some stock on hand, reduce the finished stock by two thirds. Let the remaining stock cool, and freeze in ice-cube trays. Then simply toss one or two cubes into your sauces as required.

Whether the restaurant is a low-cost Indian takeaway or an upmarket Indian restaurant, the chefs will normally stew red meat for curries before service so that it is tender and ready to use. The reason for this is simple: if they didn't, it would take too long to serve their delicious curries.

Lamb, mutton and hoofed game require about 1–1½ hours to cook and become tender using this method. These animals need a lot of exercise so their muscly flesh is naturally tough. Beef will be tender in about 40 minutes to 1 hour. Cows are quite lazy, after all.

Whatever you do, don't rush things. Stew the meat until it is good and tender. By the way, this pre-cooked lamb recipe is actually a mouth-watering curry in its own right. Lamb is the most popular red meat used in curry houses, so I've used it here, but feel free to experiment with the red meat of your choice.

PRE-COOKED STEWED LAMB/MEAT

MAKES ENOUGH FOR ABOUT 10 SERVINGS

2 tbsp rapeseed oil
6 cloves
5 black cardamom or 10 green cardamom pods, lightly bruised
10 black peppercorns
1 tbsp cumin seeds
1 tbsp coriander seeds
5cm (2in) piece of cinnamon stick or cassia bark
1 piece of mace
3 Indian bay leaves (cassia leaves)
2 large onions, finely chopped
½ tsp sea salt
2 tbsp ginger and garlic paste (see p18)
1kg (2¼ lb) leg of lamb, cut into 2.5cm (1in) pieces (keep the bone if you have it)
2 tbsp mild paprika
1 tsp chilli powder (optional)
1 tbsp garam masala (see p14)
Spice stock (see p18) or water

Heat the oil in a large saucepan over a medium-high heat until hot and beginning to bubble. Add the whole spices and bay leaves and stir for about 30 seconds, until your kitchen begins to fill with the delicious aroma of the frying spices, being careful not to burn them. Add the onions and stir to coat in the oil.

Cook for about 5 minutes before adding the salt followed by the garlic and ginger paste. Fry for a further minute until the onions are soft and translucent and your kitchen smells like the best curry house in the world. This only gets better! Place the leg bone (if you have it) in the pan with the ground spices and the meat.

Brown the meat for a couple of minutes then pour in just enough spice stock or water to cover. Simmer for about 1–1½ hours until the meat is good and tender.

Allow the meat and cooking sauce to cool for use in your curries. The meat and cooking stock (remove the bone, if using) can be stored in the fridge for up to 3 days and freeze well for up to 2 months. The stock is usually strained before adding to curries.

TIP: Double this recipe and you've got a nice meal for the day you cook as well as lots of tasty pre-cooked meat for your BIR curries. If serving as a curry, be sure to season it with salt to taste.

You might wonder why you would want to pre-cook keema, as I did when I first started noticing the containers of prepared keema during my restaurant visits. Keema is, after all, ground meat, so it's as tender as it's going to get. This recipe takes about 30 minutes or longer to make, so you can understand why the chefs in a busy takeaway would want to get this job done before they get busy.

That isn't the only reason though. Just like a slowly cooked Bolognese sauce, the flavours in this keema will develop as they cook. If you have the time, cook it longer with a little more stock as the flavour will only get better. If you aren't a big fan of biting into whole spices, be sure to count them in and remove them before using in your recipes. This keema is delicious stirred into almost any curry sauce or wrapped into samosas (see page 38).

PRE-COOKED LAMB KEEMA
MAKES ENOUGH FOR 4–10 SERVINGS DEPENDING ON USE

3 tbsp rapeseed or seasoned oil (see p7)
2 Indian bay leaves (cassia leaves)
7.5cm (3 in) piece of cinnamon stick or cassia bark
1 tsp cumin seeds
4 green cardamom pods, lightly bruised
½ onion, finely chopped
1 tbsp garlic and ginger paste (see p18)
1 tbsp mixed powder (see p17)
1 tbsp garam masala (see p14)
½ tsp ground turmeric
2 tbsp tomato purée (see p19)
500–700g (1–1½ lb) minced lamb or chicken
About 200ml (1 cup) spice stock (see p18) or water
1 tsp dried fenugreek (methi) leaves
3 tbsp finely chopped coriander (cilantro)
Salt

Heat the oil over a medium-high heat until small bubbles appear, then add the bay leaves, cinnamon stick, cumin seeds and cardamom pods and mix them around in the oil. After about 30 seconds the oil will become fragrant and you will hear the spices begin to crackle. When this happens, toss in the onion and give it a good stir. Fry until soft and translucent but not browned.

Add the garlic and ginger paste and let it sizzle for another minute or so, then add the ground spices and tomato purée followed by the minced meat. You'll know you're doing something right because your kitchen will smell so good.

Allow the minced meat to cook through then pour in the spice stock or water and simmer over a low heat for about 20 minutes. You may need to add a little more water while the ingredients all get to know each other. The finished keema should be moist but not saucy, and if you'd like to cook it for longer for a more intense flavour, add more water accordingly to prevent it from drying out.

Remove the bay leaves, cinnamon stick and cardamom pods. Stir in the dried fenugreek leaves, fresh coriander (cilantro) and salt to taste. You'll probably find it tastes great, so be careful not to snack on it before making your keema curry or using it in your samosas! I find this quite difficult at times.

This pre-cooked potato dish can be eaten on its own or used in other British Indian restaurant-style dishes. Serve it as is and it could be a delicious, authentic style Bombay aloo, in which case I recommend cutting the potato cubes smaller (there is also a BIR version of Bombay Aloo on page 116) in which you can use these pre-cooked potatoes. Be sure to cook the potatoes until they are soft. Nobody likes an 80% cooked, hard potato.

This is exactly why you will want to make this recipe if you are intending on whipping up a potato-based curry or two. It's a good job to get done early so that all you have to do is heat them up in the curry sauce of your choice and serve. They keep for at least 3 days, covered in the fridge and can also be frozen with their tasty cooking stock. Defrost before using.

PRE-COOKED STEWED POTATOES
MAKES ENOUGH FOR 4 SERVINGS*

2 tbsp rapeseed or
    seasoned oil (see p7)
1 tbsp ghee
1 tsp brown mustard seeds
1 tbsp cumin seeds
7.5cm (3in) piece of cinnamon
    stick or cassia bark
5 green cardamom pods,
    lightly bruised
3 large onions, finely sliced
2 tbsp garlic and ginger paste
    (see p18)
1 x 400g tin (2 cups) chopped
    tomatoes
1 tbsp Kashmiri mild chilli
    powder, or to taste
1 tsp ground turmeric
500g (1 lb) potatoes, peeled
    and each cut into 3
650ml (2¾ cups) spice stock
    (see p18) or water
1 tbsp garam masala (see p14)
Salt and freshly ground pepper

*This is one of those "How Long Is a Piece of String?" recipes. The idea is to cook as many or as few potatoes as you need for the recipe(s) you want to use them in.

Heat the oil and ghee over a high heat in a large saucepan then throw in the mustard seeds. When they begin to pop, reduce the heat to medium high and toss in the cumin seeds, cinnamon stick and cardamom pods, and temper in the oil for a further 30 seconds. Stir in the onions and fry for about 5 minutes until soft and translucent, stirring regularly, then add the garlic and ginger paste and let it sizzle in the oil for about 1 minute. Tip in the tomatoes, chilli powder and turmeric, and stir it all up nicely.

Now add the potato pieces and cover with the spice stock or water. Cover and simmer until the potatoes are soft and cooked through, about 30 minutes. Sprinkle with the garam masala and salt and pepper to taste, and give it all a good stir. Serve the potatoes as they are immediately or remove the potato pieces and strain the stock for use in your curries. This will keep for at least 3 days in the fridge and can also be frozen. The strained cooking stock adds a nice flavour to vegetarian curries.

TIP: If serving this as a dish on its own, you might like to spice it up a bit by adding chilli powder and/or chopped green chillies to taste. Garnish with chopped fresh coriander (cilantro).

Paneer is often added raw to curries just before serving, as you can't cook it in a sauce long or it will begin to break up. Here is another option. The crispy exterior that the paneer gets when shallow-fried helps stop it from disintegrating in the sauce, and it's also delicious. Plain paneer doesn't have a lot of flavour so marinating for about a half hour before frying will make it more interesting.

I find commercially available paneer works perfectly well for BIR curries, frying and grilling but I also like to make my own. To do this, bring 1.5 litres (6 cups) of full-fat milk to a boil, whisking continuously so that it doesn't boil over. When the milk has come to a boil, lower the heat and simmer to reduce by about 15%. Remove the milk from the heat and stir in the juice of one lemon and whisk for five to ten minutes to separate the curds from the whey.

Wrap the curds tightly in cheesecloth and hang over the sink for about two hours. Form the paneer into a block, pressing out any remaining whey and you've got the 200g of fresh paneer needed for this recipe! Your homemade paneer will keep in the fridge for up to three days.

FRIED PANEER
SERVES 4–10 DEPENDING ON USE

1 tsp garlic and ginger paste
　(see p18)
½ tsp chilli powder
½ tsp garam masala (see p14)
1 tbsp Greek yoghurt
200g (1½ cups) paneer
　(see above for homemade),
　cubed
3 tbsp rapeseed oil
Salt

Whisk the garlic and ginger paste, spices and yoghurt together in a bowl. Using a fork or toothpick, pierce the paneer cubes all over so that the marinade can penetrate. Add the paneer and leave to marinate for about 30 minutes.

When ready to fry, heat the oil in a frying pan over a medium-high heat. When it begins to bubble, remove the paneer from the marinade and add to the hot oil. Fry until browned on one side, then flip the paneer over and fry on the other side. Only frying two opposite sides is enough to help keep the cheese together while cooking in a sauce, but if you like you can brown it on all sides, as I do (it just looks better).

Transfer the browned paneer cubes to a plate lined with kitchen paper, to absorb any excess oil, and set aside until ready to use.

Most British Indian restaurant-style curry sauces are very smooth. Sometimes though, the curry needs just a bit more crunch – curries such a dry bhunas and spicy jalfrezis, for example. Adding a spoonful of this pre-cooked onion and pepper mixture will do just that.

In many of the curry houses I've visited, there is a tub of cooked onions and other vegetables at the ready for when they are needed. As they are already pre-cooked, they can be added to a curry at the end of cooking. The veggies can be stored in the fridge for up to 3 days.

Is this necessary? I don't think so for the home cook as vegetables cook very quickly anyway, as many of my recipes demonstrate. If you're cooking for a large group of people, however, you might like to have these fried veggies on hand. Add them to any curry you want even if not suggested in the recipe. If you like crunchy veggies in your curries, you really can't go wrong.

STIR-FRIED ONIONS AND OTHER VEGGIES

MAKES ENOUGH FOR 4–10 SERVINGS DEPENDING ON USE

2 tbsp rapeseed oil or seasoned oil skimmed from the base curry sauce (see p7)
1 tsp panch poran (see p16)
4 onions, finely sliced
1 green pepper (bell pepper), deseeded and thinly sliced
1 red pepper (bell pepper), deseeded and thinly sliced
Pinch of ground turmeric

Heat the oil in a large pan over a medium-high heat. Toss in the panch poran and sizzle for about 10 seconds before adding the onions and peppers (bell peppers). Fry for about 10 minutes until soft but the peppers still have a nice crunch to them.

Add the turmeric and stir to combine. Tip into a bowl to cool and use as required. This same method can also be used for other vegetables.

STARTERS

Almost everyone loves a papadam or two while eagerly awaiting their curry dinner. Most good Indian restaurants fry their own as they are much better than those pre-packed papadams found at supermarkets. If you happen upon a restaurant that doesn't fry their own in-house, it is a good sign that you should make a quick exit.

The great news is that papadams aren't difficult to prepare. Many supermarkets and Asian food shops sell papads, which are flat lentil discs that when fried turn into lovely papadams. You could also purchase papad flour and make your own. I did once and won't again. Ready-made papads are the way to go.

Papads are available plain or with whole spices – I love cumin papads, black pepper papads and chilli papads. If you can find these, be sure to give them a try.

Use a pan that is at least 4cm (1½ in) wider in diameter to the papads you are using as they do expand.

PAPADAMS

Rapeseed oil, for deep-frying
Papads (1–2 per person)

Heat 10cm (4 in) of oil in a large pan or wok until hot. When a piece of papad puffs up quite quickly when dropped into the oil, it's ready. Papads are usually cooked in pairs, which speeds the process up and also helps keep them uniformly flat. Drop the papads in the oil. They will very quickly expand into full-sized papadams. Be careful not to overcook or burn the papadams. They will quickly begin to turn brown, so remove them from the oil before this happens. It only takes seconds to overcook papadams, so be ready to get them out of that oil. Remove from the oil with tongs or a wire mesh spoon and place on kitchen paper to absorb the excess oil.

You can leave them to cool flat, or fold them into your own preferred shapes while they are still hot. Serve or store in an airtight container.

TIP: When I am planning a curry night in with friends, I cook papadams earlier in the day so that I can check them off the to-do list. This is what they do at busy restaurants too, often making enough for 3 or more days in one go.

You won't find bora and podina on many curry-house menus but I think they're missing a trick. This is Bangladeshi snack food and an excellent alternative to papadams. It does take a little longer to make but it's worth every extra minute.

This recipe was emailed to me by Eshan 'Mo' Miah. Mo and I have never met face to face but I feel like we're great friends. Back in the early days of my blog, Mo started sending me his family recipes as well as recipes from his family's restaurant, Table Talk, which is local to me. At the time, Mo was living and working near London but he arranged for me to visit the Table Talk kitchen to learn from his father, Manik Miah. I picked up so many tips and recipes that day.

Mo has been a great source for recipes, a few of which you'll find in this book. He recently opened a new restaurant in Newquay called Zaman's. If it is anywhere near as good as Table Talk, he's on to a winner!

BORA AND PODINA
MAKES ENOUGH FOR 4 AS A SNACK

FOR THE BORA
100g (½ cup) masoor dhal (orange lentils)
½ onion, finely chopped
1 tsp salt
½ tsp ground turmeric
380g (3 cups) rice flour
Rapeseed oil, for deep-frying

FOR THE PODINA
½ bunch of fresh mint
½ bunch of fresh coriander (cilantro)
10–15 fresh green chillies, to taste
420g (2 cups) plain yoghurt
Salt

For the podina, put the mint, coriander (cilantro), chillies and 2 tbsp water in a blender and blitz to a paste. Add this to the yoghurt in a bowl and mix until smooth, adding salt to taste. Refrigerate until really cold.

For the bora, wash the lentils and soak them in cold water for 30 minutes. Drain and transfer to a saucepan. Add 550ml (2 cups) fresh water, the onion, salt and turmeric. Cook over a medium heat until the lentils are soft and the water is almost all gone.

Tip the lentils into a bowl and stir in the rice flour. Mix thoroughly with your hands until you have a smooth dough (mixing everything while still warm makes it easier).

On a flat surface, roll out the dough to a 2–3mm (¹⁄₁₆ in) thickness (separate the dough into smaller balls to make this easier if you like). Cut out bite-sized pieces of the dough, either in long triangles or use cookie cutters to make different shapes.

Heat at least 10cm (4 in) of rapeseed oil in a heavy-based pan for deep frying. When a piece of dough sizzles immediately when dropped into the oil, about 170°C/338°F, you're read to cook. Fry in batches, transfer to a plate lined with kitchen paper and keep warm while you deep-fry the rest. Season with a little more salt to taste if you like. They are ideally served piping hot with the fridge-cold podina.

Shop-bought filo pastry is most often used at Indian restaurants. It does the job, but there's nothing like homemade so I have included my pastry recipe here. If you want to make these samosas ahead of time, you can freeze them once shaped but not fried, on a plate, wrapped tightly in cling film (plastic wrap). Once frozen, transfer to a freezer bag and store until ready to fry, defrosting them first.

LAMB OR VEGETABLE SAMOSAS

MAKES 18–20

Rapeseed oil, for deep-frying

FOR THE PASTRY
400g (3 cups) plain
    (all-purpose) flour
Pinch of salt
1 tbsp rapeseed oil
1 tbsp melted ghee

FOR THE MEAT FILLING
1 quantity pre-cooked keema
    (see p28)*

FOR VEGETABLE FILLING
2 tbsp rapeseed oil
1 tsp cumin seeds
1 onion, finely chopped
2 green bird's-eye chillies,
    finely chopped
1 tbsp garlic and ginger paste
    (see p18)
2 floury potatoes, peeled and
    cut into 1cm (½ in) cubes
2 tsp mixed powder (see p17)
About 250ml (1 cup) homemade
    vegetable stock or spice stock
    (see p18) Enough to cover
1 carrot, finely chopped
3 tbsp finely chopped fresh
    coriander (cilantro)
125g (1 cup) frozen peas
Salt

*You will probably have some keema left over. Go ahead and use it in a curry or refrigerate/freeze for later use.

Mix 350g (2⅔ cups) of the flour in a large bowl with the salt, oil and ghee. Slowly drizzle enough water into the mixture until you have a firm but sticky dough. Sprinkle the remaining flour on a clean surface, tip out the dough and knead until it no longer sticks to your hands, about 5 minutes. Cover the dough and let rest for 30 minutes.

To make the vegetable filling, heat the oil in a large pan over a medium-high heat until bubbles appear. Add the cumin seeds. When they become fragrant in the oil, toss in the onion and chillies, and fry until the onion is translucent and lightly browned. Add the garlic and ginger paste and fry for a further minute.

Add the potatoes and mixed powder, and just enough water or spice stock to cover. Simmer until the potatoes are soft, topping up the stock if needed. Add the carrot and continue cooking until cooked through but still al dente . Reduce the stock until you have a dry potato mixture. Stir in the chopped coriander (cilantro) and peas and add salt to taste. Set aside to cool.

Tear off a piece of dough the size of a golf ball and place on a floured surface (keep the remaining dough in the bowl covered so that it doesn't dry out). Roll the dough into a very thin rectangle, the thinner the better, about 5 × 12cm (2 × 4½ in).

To make your lamb or vegetable samosas, place about 1 tbsp filling at the top of the pastry rectangle. Fold the top left corner over the filling to make a small triangular pocket. There will still be about 6cm (2½ in) pastry under this triangular pocket. Fold the top of the triangle over onto the remaining pastry and then again to create a little triangular samosa. Press the seams together tightly and repeat until all of the samosas are made.

When ready to cook pour 10cm (4 in) of rapeseed oil into a deep saucepan and heat to 170°C/338°F. Fry the samosas in batches until nicely browned. Remove with a slotted spoon to a rack and keep warm while you fry the rest of the samosas.

I first tried making this recipe after a visit to a restaurant called Simla in Dordon near Tamworth. Mohammed Nanu, the owner, asked his head chef to make several dishes for me, knowing I needed ideas for this book. They served this crab in deep-fried pastry shells and it was so good. I decided to use the crab filling for samosas. I think my friends at Simla will approve. Try dipping these into the honey mustard raita on page 145.

CRAB SAMOSAS
MAKES 18–20

1 quantity homemade
   samosa pastry (see opposite)
Rapeseed oil, for deep-frying

FOR THE CRAB FILLING
2 tbsp rapeseed oil
1 tsp mustard seeds
10 fresh curry leaves,
   finely chopped
½ onion, finely chopped
1 tbsp garlic and ginger paste
   (see p18)
½ tsp salt
1 tbsp mixed powder (see p17)
½ tsp chilli powder
3½ tbsp tomato purée (see p19)
4 tbsp spice stock (see p18)
   or water
250g (1 cup) fresh white
   crabmeat
1 tsp soy sauce

To make the crab filling, heat the oil in a frying pan until bubbly hot. Sprinkle in the mustard seeds and, when they begin to pop, stir in the curry leaves and onion, and fry until the onion is soft and translucent. Add the garlic and ginger paste and the salt and mix it all up in the pan for about 30 seconds. Stir in the mixed powder, chilli powder and tomato purée, along with the spice stock or water.

Let this sizzle for about a minute and then pour it all into a bowl. Stir in the crabmeat (it will already be cooked) and the soy sauce. Check for seasoning.

Roll out the pastry as described opposite and use the crab filling to shape into samosas. Either freeze at this stage, or set aside until ready to cook.

Deep-fry the samosas in batches following the method opposite and serve with the honey mustard raita (page 145).

Onion bhajis and vegetable pakora are best cooked in two stages. The first cooking is in oil that is hot enough to sizzle and cook them through. The bhajis are then removed to rest and the oil temperature is increased. The cooked bhajis are then fried again in the hotter oil to give them a darker and crispier exterior.

Mixing the sliced onions with salt at the beginning of the recipe is key to making the perfect bhajis. If you were to bend a fresh onion slice, it would snap. The salt releases moisture from the onion slices so that they become limp and no longer snap when bent. This makes it easier to form your bhajis. See photograph on page 37.

ONION BHAJIS
SERVES 4–8

3 onions (slightly larger than tennis balls), sliced
1 tsp fine sea salt
4 tbsp rice flour
140g (1 cup) chickpea (gram) flour
1 tbsp garlic paste (see p18)
2.5cm (1in) piece of ginger, peeled and cut into matchsticks
2 fresh green chillies, roughly chopped
1 tbsp panch poran (see p16)
2 tbsp rapeseed oil, plus extra for deep-frying
3 tbsp finely chopped coriander (cilantro) leaves

Place the sliced onions in a bowl, sprinkle over the salt and mix it all up with your hands to ensure the onions are evenly coated with the salt. Let them sit for 30 minutes or up to 2 hours; the salt will release the moisture from the onions, which will become part of your batter.

When ready to form your bhajis, sift the flours over the onions and add the garlic paste, ginger, chillies, panch poran, 2 tbsp oil and coriander (cilantro). Begin to work these ingredients into the sliced onions with your hands until they are nicely coated. There should be enough moisture from the onions and oil, but if you are finding it a bit too sticky, add just a little water. When you can easily form a bhaji with your hands, you're ready to go.

Heat about 10cm (4 in) of rapeseed oil to 160°C/320°F in a large pan. Form the onion mixture into bhajis about the size of golf balls, or larger if you prefer. Fry in small batches until lightly browned and cooked through, then remove them with a slotted spoon to a rack to rest while you fry the rest of your bhajis.

When all the bhajis are cooked, raise the heat of the oil to 180°C/356°F and fry them again in small batches until you are happy with the colour of the exterior. Serve immediately or, if working ahead, place the bhajis on a rack placed over a foil-lined dish in a low oven for up to 30 minutes.

OTHER IDEAS: You can make vegetable pakoras in the same way, adding whatever vegetable you like to the mix. Broccoli and cauliflower cut into small pieces both work well. Diced potatoes, chopped green chillies, courgettes (zucchini) and aubergines (eggplants) are also good.

Back in 2012, I was invited to Sachins in Newcastle by the owner and excellent chef Bob Arora. That day he taught me a few authentic Punjabi recipes that I still make often. This potato kofta recipe is one of them.

I usually serve these koftas with a selection of other starters when we have people over. The koftas and sauce make a delicious vegetarian curry but I like to serve them as canapés. To do this, spoon some of the hot yoghurt sauce into small canapé dishes and place a potato kofta with a toothpick on top. Scoop up the hot sauce with the crunchy koftas and you'll understand why I had to share this recipe.

POTATO KOFTAS
WITH A SPICY YOGHURT SAUCE

SERVES 4 AS A MAIN COURSE OR MANY AS A CANAPÉ

3 large potatoes
Pinch of ground turmeric
Pinch of salt
1 tsp finely chopped
   coriander seeds
1 tbsp garam masala (see p14)
Handful of fresh coriander
   (cilantro), chopped
2–3 tbsp self-raising
   (self-rising) flour
Rapeseed oil, for deep-frying

FOR THE SAUCE
420g (2 cups) plain yoghurt
1 tsp chilli powder
1 tsp ground turmeric
1 tbsp tomato paste
1 tsp cornflour (cornstarch)
   (optional)
Pinch of salt
2 tbsp rapeseed oil
1 tsp chopped coriander seeds
1 tsp mustard seeds
6 fenugreek seeds
10 fresh curry leaves
3 tbsp finely chopped fresh
   coriander (cilantro)

Boil the potatoes in their skins until about 80% cooked, then drain. When cool enough to handle, peel then grate them into a large bowl. Stir in the turmeric, salt, chopped coriander seeds, garam masala, fresh coriander (cilantro) and 2 tbsp flour. Form into koftas the size of golf balls, adding more flour if the mix is too sticky.

Now make the sauce. Pour the yoghurt into a large bowl and add the chilli powder, turmeric, tomato paste, cornflour (cornstarch) and salt. Whisk until smooth. Heat the oil over a medium-high heat and toss in the whole spices followed by the curry leaves. Sizzle for about 20 seconds until fragrant and then slowly pour in the yoghurt mixture, whisking continuously. The yoghurt may splatter a bit when it hits the oil, so reduce the heat if necessary.

Whisk it all up and simmer for about 3 minutes, then skim the excess oil off the top. Set aside and keep warm.

Heat about 10 cm (4 in) of rapeseed oil in a deep, heavy-based pan, until hot enough for a piece of the potato mixture to sizzle immediately it hits the oil (about 170°C/338°F). Deep-fry the koftas in batches of six until nicely browned and crunchy on the outside. Remove to a plate lined with kitchen paper, to absorb any excess oil, then move to a wire rack and keep warm while you fry the rest.

Check the sauce for seasoning. If serving as a curry, stir the kofta into the sauce and serve immediately while still crunchy, or serve as an hors d'oeuvre, placing each kofta on top of a spoonful of sauce.

You can't beat a good prawn (shrimp) butterfly. They may not be good for you but they are quite moreish and worth every calorie. I recommend using the largest prawns you can find – they are easier to prepare and there is a lot more to them.

If you are serving these to friends as part of a multi-dish curry feast, heat your oven to about 150°C/300°F/gas mark 2 and fry them a good half hour before everyone arrives, placing them on a rack placed over a foil-lined dish in the oven. Then simply transfer them from the oven to a warm plate to serve.

PRAWN BUTTERFLY

MAKES 8–10

8–10 unpeeled raw large
   prawns (shrimp)
4 tbsp chickpea (gram) flour
2 tbsp rice flour
1 tbsp baking powder
½ tsp roasted cumin seeds
   (see p12)
1 tbsp mixed powder (see p17)
1 tsp chilli powder or to taste
Salt
Rapeseed oil, for deep-frying

Using a sharp knife, slice down the centre of the back of each prawn (shrimp) and remove the black or clear vein. Peel off the head and the rest of the shell down to the tail. Leave the tail intact as it makes a good and attractive handle. Continue to make a shallow incision into the back to butterfly each prawn. Place cling film (plastic wrap) over the butterflied prawns and lightly pound them flat with a mallet.

For the batter, mix the flours, baking powder, cumin, mixed powder and chilli powder together in a bowl. Slowly whisk in about 125ml (½ cup) water, until you have a batter the consistency of double (heavy) cream and thick enough to coat the back of a spoon but slowly drip off. If it is too thick, add a little more water or a pinch more gram flower if too thin. Season the batter with salt to taste.

Heat about 15 cm (6 in) of rapeseed oil in a deep, heavy-based pan or wok, until hot enough for a drop of batter to sizzle immediately when dropped in the oil. Dip and coat your prawns with the batter, slowly lower each battered prawn into the hot oil and fry for about 3 minutes until nicely browned on the exterior and cooked through. You might need to do this in batches.

If cooking ahead (see introduction) remove to a cooling rack placed over a foil-lined dish for any excess oil to drain off, and place in the warm oven (they will stay nice and crisp for 30 minutes).

TIP: These are great served with my pakora sauce (see page 144).

Chicken pakora is served in so many different ways at restaurants across the UK. The chicken breast meat can be cut into long strips or simple bite-sized cubes that are perfect served as finger food. Often, the meat is dyed bright red to make it look spicy hot, although usually it's not very spicy at all.

After trying many different possibilities, I decided to revisit my friend Bob Arora's recipe from Sachins in Newcastle. It's simple but the spices all work together so well. Bob only recommends ½ tsp chilli powder, but I added a whole teaspoon because I like my pakoras on the spicy side. I'll leave that one up to you.

I like to serve this Indian fried chicken with coriander, garlic and chilli raita (page 145). You might like it with that sweet-and-sour red sauce that pakoras are often served with, and I have included a nice one on page 144. It's so good!

The chicken pakoras in the accompanying photo were made by cutting the chicken into very small cubes and then squeezing them together in the batter. These really went down a treat once the photo was taken.

CHICKEN PAKORA
SERVES 2 OR 4 AS PART OF A MULTI-COURSE MEAL

250g (1½ cup) boneless chicken breast, cubed or sliced
½ tsp ground turmeric
½ tsp ajwain (carom) seeds
¾ tsp garam masala (see p14)
½–1 tsp chilli powder, to taste
¾ tsp garlic and ginger paste (see p18)
2 tbsp finely chopped coriander (cilantro)
White of 1 small egg
65g (½ cup) chickpea (gram) flour
Sparkling water
Rapeseed oil, for deep-frying
Salt
Lemon wedges, onion rings and lettuce, to serve

Place the chicken in a large bowl and mix with the turmeric, ajwain, garam masala, chilli powder and a little salt so that the meat is evenly coated. Let this sit for about 20 minutes.

Stir in the garlic and ginger paste, coriander (cilantro) and the egg white. Now start adding the chickpea (gram) flour a little at a time, coating the meat, adding a splash of sparkling water from time to time. Continue until all the flour is used up and it has the consistency of ketchup.

Heat enough oil for deep-frying in a deep, heavy-based pan or deep-fat fryer, to between 170 and 180°C (338–356°F). Using a wire mesh spoon, slowly lower the pakora into the hot oil. You may need to fry in batches and cooking times will of depend on the size of your chicken chunks, but it should only take a few minutes to cook through.

One of the things about making Indian food daily and then blogging about it is that inevitably you come across recipes you want to make all the time. Tandoori chicken legs are a family favourite and my basic recipe has changed very little over the years.

Red food colouring is often added to the chicken to give it that familiar appearance, but it is being used a lot less these days – it adds no flavour and is solely there for appearance.

TANDOORI CHICKEN LEGS
SERVES 4 OR MORE AS PART OF A MULTI-COURSE MEAL

8 chicken legs, including
    the thigh, skinned
Juice of 2 limes
1 tsp salt
1 tsp red food colouring powder
    (optional, see introduction)

FOR THE MARINADE
100g (½ cup) Greek yoghurt
1 tbsp ground cumin
3 tbsp garlic and ginger paste
    (see p18)
1 tsp ground coriander
1 tsp garam masala (see p14)
1 tsp tandoori masala (see p15)
1 tsp chilli powder
1 tbsp green chilli paste
    (see p18)
½ tsp amchoor (dried
    mango powder)

Cut 3–5 shallow slits in each chicken leg and place in a large bowl. Squeeze the lime juice over the chicken and rub it into the meat along with the salt and the red food colouring, if using. Set aside while you make the marinade.

Place all the marinade ingredients in a bowl and work them together with your hands until smooth. Cover the chicken with the marinade and allow to marinate for at least 2 hours, or up to 48 hours; the longer the better.

When ready to cook, skewer the chicken legs onto flat skewers and heat your barbecue. Grill using the direct grilling method (see page 88) until the chicken is nicely charred and then turn. This is important when using skewers, as the meat needs to cook so that it expands and doesn't move around on the skewers.

If you can't be bothered to fire up the barbecue? No worries! Preheat your oven to 200°C/400°F/gas mark 6 and cook the chicken on a rack placed over a foil-lined oven tray for about 20 minutes or until cooked through. To get a nice black char, you can finish the cooked chicken directly under the grill (broiler) heated to maximum temperature, for a minute or so.

Kashmiri lamb cutlets are irresistible; cooking the meat in the spiced milk makes them melt-in-the-mouth tender. The succulent pieces of lamb can be eaten by hand like chicken nuggets ... I bet you can't eat just one.

I've used boned lamb chops for this recipe but any good meaty lamb cut will do. You could even cut the chops in half if you are serving a selection of starters to a group.

KASHMIRI LAMB CUTLETS
SERVES 4 OR MORE AS PART OF A MULTI-COURSE MEAL

12 lamb chops
500ml (2 cups) full-fat milk
2.5cm (1in) piece of cinnamon
 stick or cassia bark
6 green cardamom pods,
 lightly bruised
1 tsp cloves
2.5cm (1in) piece of ginger,
 peeled and grated
1 large onion, finely chopped
1 tsp ground cumin
1 tsp freshly ground black
 pepper
1 tbsp mixed powder (see p17)
Rapeseed or vegetable oil,
 for deep-frying

FOR THE BATTER
4 tbsp chickpea (gram) flour
1 tbsp baking powder
1 tbsp rice flour
1 tbsp chilli powder
150g (⅔ cup) plain yoghurt
1 tsp garam masala (see p14)
Pinch of salt
Flaky sea salt and 3 limes,
 quartered, to serve

Remove the bone from the chops and pound the meat with a meat mallet into small, flat steaks. Place in the fridge until ready to use.

Pour the milk into a saucepan and add the cinnamon, seeds from the cardamom pods, cloves, ginger, onion, cumin, pepper and mixed powder. Bring to a boil, then add the meat to the milk mixture and simmer for 30 minutes. Remove the meat from the milk and pat dry with kitchen paper.

Now whisk the batter ingredients together. It should be quite thick, like double (heavy) cream, so that it clings to the cutlets, so add a little more chickpea (gram) flour if it is too thin or more yoghurt if too thick.

Heat about 15cm (6 in) of rapeseed oil in a deep, heavy-based pan or wok, until a little batter dropped in sizzles immediately (about 170°C/338°F). Coat one of the lamb cutlets with the batter and slowly ease it into the oil. Repeat with the rest of the meat, but don't overload your pan – you may need to cook the lamb in batches.

Deep-fry until nicely browned then remove with a wire mesh spoon to a plate lined with kitchen paper, to soak up any excess oil. Sprinkle with a little flaky sea salt and serve with the lime wedges. They are also great dipped into your favourite raita or chutney.

TIP: If cooking ahead of time, you can place the finished cutlets on a wire rack placed over a foil-lined baking tray in a low oven, for up to 30 minutes.

When you bite into these shami kebabs, they simply melt in your mouth. Crisp on the exterior and fall-apart tender inside, I can't get enough of them. Although I use lamb for this recipe, mutton is a popular alternative. If you've got the bone from the shoulder, simmer it with the meat for even more fantastic flavour.

Shami kebabs are wonderful formed into small patties as a starter course. There are few things as toothsome as a hot shami drizzled with coriander (cilantro) garlic and chilli raita or spicy tomato chutney. They are also delicious wrapped up in warm naans as a main course. As most of the work is done ahead of time, you only need to fry them up for a couple minutes and dinner is served!

LAMB SHAMI KEBABS
SERVES 6 OR MORE AS PART OF A MULTI-COURSE MEAL

1kg (2¼ lb) lamb shoulder, roughly chopped and trimmed of excess fat
150g (scant 1 cup) chana dhal, rinsed and soaked for 30 minutes
3 tbsp garlic and ginger paste (see p18)
3 Kashmiri dried red chillies
1 onion, roughly chopped
2 tsp mixed powder (see p17)
2 tsp garam masala (see p14)
Small bunch of coriander (cilantro)
2 tbsp chopped mint leaves
2 green bird's-eye chillies, or to taste
Rapeseed oil, for shallow-frying
2 large eggs, beaten
Salt

Place the lamb in a large saucepan, add water to cover and bring to the boil, skimming off the foam that rises to the top. Add the chana dhal, garlic and ginger paste, dried chillies, onion and mixed powder.

Cover and simmer for about an hour until the water evaporates and the meat is fork tender, stirring in the garam masala after 45 minutes. Watch the pan carefully so that the dhal doesn't scorch on the bottom, adding more water if required.

Allow to cool, then transfer the mixture to a food processor with the fresh coriander (cilantro), mint and chillies. Blend until fine, with the consistency of thick clay. Add salt to taste and form into patties. This can all be done well ahead of serving.

When ready to fry, heat enough oil for shallow-frying in a large frying pan. Brush both sides of each patty with the beaten egg, place in the hot oil and cook until browned, about 1 minute per side. Remove from the oil to a plate lined with kitchen paper.

THE
CLASSIC
BRITISH
CURRIES

I hope you enjoy making these classic curries as much as I do. Here you will find recipes for the most popular versions, but you can add whatever you like to the individual sauces. You can substitute different vegetables, meat, poultry, seafood and paneer, just like when you dine out at your favourite Indian restaurant.

There are no rules. If you fancy a naga goat korma, then add some pre-cooked goat tikka and naga chillies to the korma sauce. If you want crunchy vegetables in your chicken chilli garlic, sauté your vegetables of choice in the hot oil before adding the other ingredients, like I do in the jalfrezi sauce, or add some pre-cooked vegetables (see page 33) at the end of cooking. The possibilities are endless and it can be fun to experiment. Here is a list of tips for adding each:

ADDING RED MEAT AND POULTRY

All of the classic curry recipes have been developed so that you can cook and serve your finished curry in about 10 minutes. To do this, you can choose from the pre-cooked tandoori or stewed meat and poultry recipes I've included in the book (see pages 26–27). You aren't limited to these, though. You could add leftover pieces of meat or roast potatoes from Sunday dinner. Leftovers never tasted so good! You could even add the meat or poultry raw. Chicken cooks through quite quickly, but if using raw red meat, be prepared to add some more water or base curry sauce and let the sauce simmer until the meat is tender.

ADDING SEAFOOD

Seafood cooks in no time. Simply add it raw to the simmering sauce and let it cook through. You can add full fillets of fish or tikka (bite-sized pieces), whatever you fancy. If adding as tikka, I recommend using meatier fish such as cod and halibut. Marinated raw and grilled tandoori prawns (shrimp) could also be added, which taste amazing.

ADDING PANEER

Paneer heats through in a sauce fast. Be careful not to overcook it as it tends to disintegrate. I recommend adding it just before serving the curry; 2 minutes in the hot sauce should do the job. I have included a recipe for pan-fried paneer (see page 30) which will keep its form better in the sauce.

ADDING VEGETABLES

Vegetables can be added in a number of ways. In the jalfrezi recipe, for example, they are quickly fried when you start making the sauce. If you are cooking for a large group of veggie fanatics, you might like to try my pre-cooked vegetable recipe (see page 33) which will speed things up. Grilled, fried and steamed vegetables are also nice in the sauces. Just add them to the sauce right before serving so that you don't over-cook them.

PLANNING AHEAD

Whether you are making just one of these curries or several, it is a good idea to get all the ingredients for each curry ready. I group the ingredients for each curry so that I have them at the ready before cooking. These curries are cooked fast over a high heat so you don't want to be looking for an ingredient or chopping onions once you get stuck in!

ADDING BASE CURRY SAUCE AND STOCK

The amount of base curry sauce and stock added in the following recipes is exactly as the measures I use at home. You may need to experiment. If you prefer a thicker sauce, let the base sauce and stock reduce. If you prefer more sauce or stock, add it and adjust seasoning accordingly. You really can't go wrong.

When people order a chicken tikka masala, they know what they want, and if it isn't just like they expect it to be, you can see the disappointment in their faces. The thing is, there are hundreds of recipes for this world-famous curry, but this BIR combo should get you the result you're looking for.

Some chefs add loads of coconut flour or block coconut whereas others leave the coconut out. Many people like this curry super sweet whereas others prefer it to be more savoury. So please use this, my favourite version, as a guide, adjusting the sweetness and coconut flavour to taste. Be sure to use tandoori chicken tikka (see page 92) for this one!

CHICKEN TIKKA MASALA

SERVES 4 OR MORE AS PART OF A MULTI-COURSE MEAL

4 tbsp ghee, rapeseed oil
   or seasoned oil (see p7)
2 tbsp garlic and ginger paste
   (see p18)
1 tbsp sugar, or to taste
2 tbsp ground almonds
2 tbsp coconut flour (optional)
6 tbsp tomato purée (see p19)
2 tbsp mixed powder
   (see p17)
2 tbsp tandoori masala
   (see p15)
1 tbsp sweet paprika
700ml (3 cups) base curry
   sauce (see p22), heated
About 125ml (½ cup) cooking
   stock or spice stock (see p18),
   (optional)
800g (1¾lb) grilled chicken
   tikka (see p92)
200ml (scant 1 cup) single
   (light) cream, plus a little
   more to finish
1 tbsp red food colouring
   powder (optional)
Juice of 1 lemon
Small bunch of fresh coriander
   (cilantro), chopped
1 tbsp dried fenugreek (methi)
   leaves
1 tsp garam masala (see p14)
Salt

Heat the ghee or oil in a large pan over a medium-high heat. When small bubbles begin to appear, stir in the garlic and ginger paste; it will sizzle. Add the sugar, ground almonds and coconut flour (if using) followed by the tomato purée. This will cool the pan slightly.

Swirl this all together into one big happy tomato party then stir in the mixed powder, tandoori masala and paprika, followed by 250ml (1 cup) of the base curry sauce. When the sauce begins to bubble, add the rest of the base curry sauce and let it simmer nicely for a few minutes. As it simmers, the sauce will begin to brown on the side of the pan. Stir this in from time to time.

If you have some cooking stock from pre-cooked stewed chicken or spice stock, you can add it for extra flavour. Add the grilled chicken to the simmering sauce to heat through.

When the sauce has cooked down to your desired thickness, add the cream and food colouring, if using, and simmer for a further couple of minutes. If the sauce becomes too thick, you can add a little more base sauce, cooking stock or spice stock.

To finish, taste and season with salt. If you like your CTMs sweet, add a little more sugar. Squeeze in the lemon juice and sprinkle with the chopped coriander (cilantro), dried fenugreek leaves and the garam masala. A swirl of cream on top adds a nice finishing touch.

NOTE: The two curries you see on the left tasted identical as they were from the same batch. The red version was done with red food colouring powder. That's how the famous bright red colour of this famous curry is achieved.

There are hundreds of recipes for authentic Indian korma. Korma, which means 'braising' in Hindi, is actually a style of cooking where meat and vegetables are braised in a sealed pot with a little liquid. The sauce can be creamy, nutty and mild like our British kormas but they can also be quite spicy and cooked in stock or water. What we know as a korma may share the same name but it isn't really a korma at all.

I prefer to use a combination of block coconut and coconut flour to give my kormas a nice coconut flavour, but you could substitute thick coconut milk, adding it with the first batch of base curry sauce and letting it cook down to your preferred consistency (you might want to reduce the amount of base curry sauce). Never use desiccated coconut or your sauce will become grainy.

My recipe will achieve a nice yellow colour as expected. You might like to add yellow food colouring powder if you desire the more intense yellow colour found at many restaurants.

CHICKEN KORMA
SERVES 4 OR MORE AS PART OF A MULTI-COURSE MEAL

4 tbsp ghee, rapeseed oil or seasoned oil (see p7)
2.5cm (1 in) piece of cinnamon stick or cassia bark
4 green cardamom pods, lightly bruised
1 tsp garlic and ginger paste (see p18)
3 tbsp sugar, or to taste
6 tbsp ground almonds
2 tbsp coconut flour
700ml (3 cups) base curry sauce (see p22)
100g (3½ oz) block coconut or 4 extra tbsp coconut flour
800g (1¾ lb) raw chicken breast, cut on the diagonal into 5mm (¼ in) slices, or pre-cooked stewed chicken (see p26)
1 tbsp garam masala (see p14)
125ml (½ cup) single (light) cream, plus a little more to finish
1 tbsp rose water or to taste
2 tbsp cold butter (optional)
Salt

Heat the ghee or oil in a large frying pan over a medium heat. When small bubbles begin to appear, toss in the cinnamon stick and cardamom pods. Let the whole spices flavour the oil for about 30 seconds then stir in the garlic and ginger paste. Fry for about 20 seconds before adding the sugar, ground almonds and coconut flour. Mix into the oil and pour in about 250ml (1 cup) of the base curry sauce; it will bubble up nicely. Break up the block coconut, if using block, and add it to the simmering sauce. It will dissolve and give your korma a nice light yellow tone.

Pour in the rest of the base curry sauce, then add the chicken. If using raw chicken, press it right into the sauce so that it cooks quickly and evenly. You can add a little more base curry sauce if you need to, as it will boil down anyway. Swirl in the garam masala.

When your chicken is cooked/heated through, remove the cardamom pods and cinnamon, and stir in the cream. Add the rose water and finish with the butter, if you want. Season with salt to taste and check the sweetness, adding more sugar if needed.

Based on the bright flavours of Sri Lanka, chicken Ceylon is a good all-rounder. I prefer it really spicy hot and add a lot more fresh chillies and chilli powder than suggested in this recipe, so feel free to do that too. I've also taken the liberty of adding a few ingredients that are rarely included in curry-house Ceylon curries but are very Sri Lankan all the same.

CHICKEN CEYLON
SERVES 4 OR MORE AS PART OF A MULTI-COURSE MEAL

4 tbsp rapeseed oil or seasoned oil (see p7)
2 star anise
7.5cm (3in) piece of cinnamon stick or cassia bark
4 green cardamom pods, bashed
20 fresh or frozen curry leaves
2 tbsp garlic and ginger paste (see p18)
2 green bird's-eye chillies, finely chopped
2 tbsp coconut flour
3 tbsp finely chopped coriander (cilantro) stalks
1 tsp Kashmiri hot chilli powder
2 tbsp mixed powder (see p17)
1 tbsp tandoori masala (see p15)
½ tbsp freshly ground black pepper
125ml (½ cup) tomato purée (see p19)
625ml (2½ cups) base curry sauce (see p22), heated
800g (1¾ lb) tandoori chicken tikka (see p92)
125ml (½ cup) spice stock (see p18) or pre-cooked stewed chicken stock (see p26)
100g (3½ oz) block coconut, cut into small pieces
1 tsp dried fenugreek (methi) leaves
2 tbsp smooth mango chutney
1–2 tbsp raw cashew paste (see p19), optional
Sugar, to taste
Juice of 1 lime
1 tsp garam masala (see p14)
3 tbsp freshly chopped coriander, to finish
Salt

Heat the oil in a large pan over a medium-high heat until it is visibly hot. Add the star anise, cinnamon stick and cardamom pods, and stir around for about 30 seconds until fragrant; be careful not to burn them. Add the curry leaves and fry for 30 seconds until their scent fills the room.

Add the garlic and ginger paste and the chopped chillies. Both will sizzle in the pan as they release their moisture and flavour into the oil. When they quieten down, after about 30 seconds, add the coconut flour and mix it all together for a few seconds before adding the coriander stalks, chilli powder, mixed powder, tandoori masala, black pepper and tomato purée.

Now stir in about 250ml (1 cup) of the base curry sauce and let it reduce for about a minute, stirring the caramelized bits into the sauce. Add the pre-cooked chicken, the rest of the base curry sauce, the stock and block coconut pieces. Let the sauce simmer for about 5 minutes until you are happy with the consistency, only stirring if it looks like it is catching on the pan.

Stir in the dried fenugreek leaves, mango chutney and cashew paste, if using. Fish out the whole spices if you want and add salt and sugar to taste. Squeeze the lime juice over the top and sprinkle with the garam masala and chopped coriander to serve.

Dopiaza curries are big on flavour and can be mild or quite spicy, depending on the restaurant. Broken down, the word *do* means two and *piaza* means onions. So the authentic Indian version of this dish is a curry with onions cooked in two different ways. If you count the base curry sauce, and fried onion petals, this recipe is made with onions cooked in four different ways so the name doesn't quite fit. That's just being technical, though.

CHICKEN DOPIAZA
SERVES 4 OR MORE AS PART OF A MULTI-COURSE MEAL

4 tbsp rapeseed oil or seasoned oil (see p7)
1 small onion, quartered and divided into petals
6 green cardamom pods, bashed
1 tsp cumin seeds
1 tsp coriander seeds, roughly chopped
3 tbsp garlic and ginger paste (see p18)
125ml (½ cup) tomato purée (see p19)
500ml (2 cups) base curry sauce (see p22), heated
600g (1 lb 5 oz) pre-cooked stewed chicken (see p26), plus 250ml (1 cup) of its cooking stock, or more base curry sauce
2 tbsp mixed powder (see p17)
1 tsp ground cumin
1–2 tsp mild or hot chilli powder, to taste
7 tbsp onion paste made with yoghurt (see p19)
1 tsp dried fenugreek (methi) leaves
Small bunch of coriander (cilantro), chopped
2 handfuls of fried onions (see p19)
1 tsp garam masala (see p14)
Salt

Heat 1 tbsp of the oil in a large pan over a high heat. When good and hot, toss in the onion petals and sear them until they are nicely charred but still quite crisp. Remove with a slotted spoon to a plate.

Reduce the heat to medium-high and pour in the rest of the oil. When bubbles start to appear, add the whole spices. Stir the spices around in the oil for about 30 seconds and enjoy the aroma of that awesome meal you're making.

Stir in the garlic and ginger paste and let it sizzle until fragrant then add the mixed powder, ground cumin, chilli powder and tomato purée. Give this all a good stir and then add 250ml (1 cup) of the base curry sauce. The curry sauce will begin to bubble rapidly and, when it does, add the rest of the sauce and the stock or extra sauce. Turn up the heat and simmer; some of the sauce may begin to caramelize on the side of the pan, so just stir this in from time to time for more flavour.

Add the chicken pieces and simmer, without stirring, for about 2 minutes, until the chicken is warmed through. The sauce will cook down and become thicker, but if it becomes too thick for your liking, add a little more chicken or spice stock or base curry sauce. Stir in the onion paste 1 tbsp at a time then the dried fenugreek leaves and charred onion petals. Add salt to taste then sprinkle with the fresh coriander (cilantro), fried onions and garam masala to serve.

Some say that chicken chasni is the new chicken tikka masala. It's sweet, not spicy, and delicious over rice or naans. For me, tandoori chicken tikka is the only way to go with this one. The flavours work so well together.

A friend of mine, Alex Wilke, worked for several years in a Glasgow Indian takeaway. He told me how customers expected their chasni curries to be bright red in colour. If they weren't the correct red, they'd be handed right back. At the takeaway, this curry was so popular, they had a glowing red chasni sauce ready to speed things up and to ensure that the chasnis were always uniform in colour. If that's the colour you prefer, you'll need some bright red food colouring powder.

CHICKEN CHASNI

SERVES 4 OR MORE AS PART OF A MULTI-COURSE MEAL

3 tbsp ghee or rapeseed oil or seasoned oil (see p7)

2 tbsp garlic and ginger paste (see p18)

½ tsp ground turmeric

500ml (2 cups) base curry sauce (see p22), heated

800g (1¾lb) pre-cooked stewed chicken (see p26), plus 125ml (½ cup) of its cooking stock, or more base curry sauce

3 tbsp smooth mango chutney (see p142)

2 tbsp mint sauce

3 tbsp tomato ketchup

1 tbsp ground cumin

200ml (scant 1 cup) double (heavy) cream

Juice of 1 or 2 lemons, to taste

Bright red food colouring powder (optional)

½ tsp garam masala (see p14)

3 tbsp very finely chopped coriander (cilantro)

Salt

Heat the ghee or oil in a large pan over a medium-high heat. When the oil is visibly hot, add the garlic and ginger paste; it will sizzle as it releases its moisture into the hot oil. Add the turmeric and fry for about 40 seconds, stirring continuously, then pour in 250ml (1 cup) of the base curry sauce. Let this come to a rapid simmer and scrape any caramelized sauce from the sides of the pan into the sauce.

Add the rest of the base sauce with the pre-cooked chicken and the stock. Let this cook for about 5 minutes, only stirring if the sauce is obviously catching on the pan, and stirring in any caramelized sauce from the side of the pan.

Stir in the mango chutney, mint sauce and ketchup followed by the cumin. Pour in the cream and simmer until good and hot. Season with salt and squeeze in the lemon juice to taste. Add red food colouring powder if you want and sprinkle with the garam masala and chopped coriander (cilantro) to serve.

Pathia curries were probably first made by Bangladeshi chefs here in Britain in an attempt to come up with an Indian dish that could compete with the sweet-and-sour chicken that was becoming popular at Chinese takeaways. It seems to have caught on because you rarely find a curry house or takeaway that doesn't have pathia on the menu.

You need to make the sauce so that it is both sweet and sour. I've seen mint sauce used as a souring agent and pineapple juice, sugar and ketchup used for sweetening. With this, my favourite combo, you get the sour flavour from the lemon and the sweetness from the sugar and mango chutney. Go ahead and adjust these ingredients to your own preferences, or even try some of the other alternative ingredients mentioned. Sometimes the best curries are discovered through a bit of experimentation.

CHICKEN PATHIA

SERVES 4 OR MORE AS PART OF A MULTI-COURSE MEAL

4 tbsp rapeseed oil or seasoned oil (see p7)
1 small onion, very finely chopped
2 tbsp garlic and ginger paste (see p18)
2 tbsp mixed powder (see p17)
1 tsp chilli powder
2 tbsp sugar
125ml (½ cup) tomato purée (see p19)
500ml (2 cups) base curry sauce (see p22) heated
800g (1¾ lb) pre-cooked stewed chicken (see p26) plus 125ml (½ cup) of its cooking stock, or more curry base sauce
1 tbsp smooth mango chutney
½ tsp tamarind concentrate
1 tsp dried fenugreek (methi) leaves
Juice of 1 or 2 lemons, to taste
3 tbsp chopped fresh coriander (cilantro)
Salt

Heat the oil in a large pan over a medium-high heat until bubbling hot. Stir in the chopped onion and fry until translucent and soft, then add the garlic and ginger paste and let it sizzle for about a minute. Then, when your kitchen smells all garlicky and gingery, sprinkle a little salt over the mixture as this will help release moisture. Cook for about another minute then add the mixed powder, chilli powder and sugar. Stir briskly.

Stir in the tomato purée and 250ml (1 cup) of the base curry sauce. Let this come to a rolling simmer and scrape back in any caramelized sauce from the sides of the pan. Add the rest of the base sauce and the stock, followed by the pre-cooked chicken. Let this bubble and spit until reduced down to your preferred consistency. Add a little more base sauce or stock if you want more sauce.

To finish, stir in the mango chutney, tamarind, dried fenugreek leaves and lemon juice to taste. Taste the curry, and if you want it to be sweeter, add some more sugar or mango chutney, or more lemon juice if you want it to have more of a tang. Check for seasoning, and add salt to taste to serve. Serve garnished with the chopped coriander (cilantro).

TIP: Prawns (shrimp) are an excellent and popular alternative to chicken.

Garlicky and spicy, chicken chilli garlic curries are one of my curry house favourites – I do love my garlic. I have experimented with this recipe many times and I think it's a winner.

It's spicy but not numbingly so. You can always add a few more chillies at the end if you want to turn the zing into a zap. By the way, if you are eating this for lunch, you probably don't want to go back to work that day. You won't be very popular.

CHICKEN CHILLI GARLIC
SERVES 4 OR MORE AS PART OF A MULTI-COURSE MEAL

4 tbsp rapeseed oil or seasoned oil (see p7)
15 garlic cloves, cut into thin slivers
1 onion, finely chopped
½ tsp salt
2 tbsp garlic and ginger paste (see p18)
3 (or more) fresh green chillies, sliced into thin rings, plus extra to serve (optional)
1 tsp chilli powder
2 tbsp mixed powder (see p17)
2 tbsp tandoori masala (see p15)
125ml (½ cup) tomato purée (see p19)
500ml (2 cups) base curry sauce (see p22), heated
800g (1¾ lb) tandoori chicken tikka (see p92) plus 125ml (½ cup) pre-cooked stewed chicken stock (see p26) or spice stock (see p18)
1 tsp dried fenugreek (methi) leaves
Salt
Small bunch of coriander (cilantro), finely chopped
Dried garlic flakes, to serve (optional)

Heat the oil in a pan over a medium heat and add the garlic slivers. It is very important not to burn the garlic, so watch the pan and move the slivers around in the pan until they become soft and are just beginning to brown.

Now add the onion and fry for about 3 minutes until soft and translucent, sprinkling a little salt over the onions to help release moisture. Stir in the garlic and ginger paste and chillies, and fry for about 20 seconds.

Increase the heat to medium-high, add the ground spices and tomato purée and sizzle for a further 30 seconds, stirring continuously. Add half the base curry sauce and bring to a rolling simmer. (You don't need to stir the sauce unless it is obviously catching on the pan.) Be sure to scrape any sauce that caramelizes on the sides of the pan back into the sauce.

Pour in the rest of the base sauce, the chicken and cooking stock and let this bubble without disturbing until the chicken is heated through and your sauce consistency is how you like it.

Stir in the dried fenugreek leaves and check for seasoning, adding salt to taste. Sprinkle with the chopped coriander (cilantro), dried garlic flakes and a few more chilli rings, if you like.

Authentic Indian pasandas can be spicy or mild, sweet and/or savoury. What makes them 'pasanda' has nothing to do with the sauces, which can vary greatly, but with the use of flattened meat, tenderized with a meat mallet before being added to the pan.

Here in the UK, our pasandas are quite similar to our kormas but usually not quite as sweet. I have yet to try one with flattened meat in a curry house, although I do use thinly sliced raw chicken rather than the standard pre-cooked chicken tikka. Either could be used. My friends at Eastern Eye in Brick Lane, London, recommend adding a splash of red wine to the sauce. Great advice! I think it really gives the sauce a unique and delicious flavour.

This curry is perfect for kids and those who aren't fans of spicy dishes.

CHICKEN PASANDA
SERVES 4 OR MORE AS PART OF A MULTI-COURSE MEAL

4 tbsp almond flakes
4 tbsp rapeseed oil or seasoned oil (see p7)
3 tbsp coconut flour
3 tbsp ground almonds
2 tbsp sugar
About 20 sultanas
500ml (2 cups) base curry sauce (see p22)
100g (3½ oz) block coconut, cut into small pieces
800g (1¾ lb) skinless, boneless chicken breast, cut into thin slices on the diagonal
A splash of red wine (125ml/ ½ cup), (optional)
100ml (1 cup) single (light) cream
1 tsp garam masala (see p14)
Salt

Toast the almond flakes in a dry pan over a medium-high heat until nicely browned. Transfer to a plate and set aside.

Add the oil to the pan. When nice and bubbly, add the coconut flour, ground almonds and sugar. Stir this around for about 30 seconds then add the sultanas, base curry sauce and block coconut pieces. When the sauce begins to simmer, stir in the chicken.

Let this simmer for about 5 minutes until the chicken is cooked through and the sauce has cooked to your preferred consistency. If the sauce caramelizes to the sides, stir it back into the sauce. At this time, you could add a splash of red wine to simmer in the sauce until the alcohol cooks out.

To serve, check for seasoning, adding salt, more coconut and sugar if desired, to taste. Stir in the cream and sprinkle with the garam masala and toasted almond flakes.

Chicken dhansak is one of the most popular curries served at curry houses around the UK. British dhansak is a play on a curry served by the Parsi community around Mumbai. There, it's usually made with goat's meat or mutton and it is a real party piece. It's traditionally served with brown rice and usually has other nice vegetables thrown in like pumpkin, aubergine (eggplant) and potato. Four different lentils are used to make the sauce along with a long list of spices.

Our British version is a lot less complicated, although it is a sweet-and-sour curry like the original. Cooked red split lentils (try my tarka dhal on page 117) are added to the sauce and it is usually sweetened with pineapple juice and chunks or rings of pineapple, and lemon juice is used as a souring agent.

CHICKEN DHANSAK

SERVES 4 OR MORE AS PART OF A MULTI-COURSE MEAL

4 tbsp rapeseed oil or seasoned oil (see p7)

2 tbsp garlic and ginger paste (see p18)

1 tsp ground turmeric

2 tbsp mixed powder (see p17)

1 tbsp chilli powder, or to taste

125ml (½ cup) tomato purée (see p19)

500ml (2 cups) base curry sauce (see p22), heated

180g (1 cup) red split lentils, rinsed and cooked in water until soft

800g (1¾lb) pre-cooked stewed chicken (see p26), plus a little of its cooking stock

115ml (scant ½ cup) pineapple juice

3–4 tinned pineapple rings, cut into pieces

Juice of 1 or 2 lemons, to taste

3 tbsp freshly chopped coriander (cilantro)

Salt

Heat the oil in a pan over a medium-high heat. Spoon in the garlic and ginger paste along with the turmeric, and let sizzle for about 30 seconds. The turmeric will become darker as you do this. Now add the mixed powder, chilli powder and tomato purée and stir briskly.

Pour in half of the base curry sauce and let it simmer for about a minute. Add the cooked lentils and stir it all up. Watch closely as lentils have a tendency to scorch on the bottom of the pan, so reduce the heat if necessary. Now add the rest of the sauce and the pre-cooked stewed chicken along with a splash of cooking stock or spice stock for additional flavour. Pour in the pineapple juice and add the pineapple pieces. Simmer for a further 3–5 minutes, adding more base curry sauce or stock if the mixture becomes too thick.

Check for seasoning and add salt to taste. Stir in the lemon juice and top with the chopped coriander (cilantro) to serve.

I visited Balti House Rishton after hearing great things about chef and owner Hussain Rashid. He invited me to come and watch him cook in person and I wasn't going to pass that offer up. I liked how he was promoting only using the freshest ingredients, so I knew I was going to be offered a good meal for my long drive, if nothing else.

He asked me what I'd like to see him prepare, and as I could see a basket full of fresh tomatoes, green bird's eye chillies, peppers and onions, I chose a jalfrezi. We sat down to one heck of a good curry and rice meal. This is my interpretation of the recipe.

Jalfrezi curries are quick stir-fries that are usually served quite dry with lots of crunchy vegetables. Of course, if you like more sauce, you're in control of that one.

CHICKEN JALFREZI
SERVES 4 OR MORE AS PART OF A MULTI-COURSE MEAL

4 tbsp rapeseed oil or seasoned oil (see p7)
1 onion, thinly sliced
1 red pepper (bell pepper), deseeded and thinly sliced
3 green bird's-eye chillies, roughly chopped
2 tbsp finely chopped coriander (cilantro) stalks
2 tbsp garlic and ginger paste (see p18)
6 tbsp tomato purée (see p19)
2 tbsp mixed powder (see p17)
1 tsp chilli powder (optional)
500ml (2 cups) base curry sauce (see p22), heated
700g (1½ lb) pre-cooked stewed chicken (see p26), plus 100ml (scant ½ cup) of its cooking stock
2 tomatoes, quartered
1 tsp dried fenugreek (methi) leaves
1 tsp garam masala (see p14)
Salt
Fresh coriander (cilantro) leaves, chopped
Green finger chillies, cut in half lengthways

Heat the oil in a large frying pan over a medium-high heat then add the sliced onion, pepper (bell pepper), green chillies and coriander (cilantro) stalks. Mix this all up in the pan and sauté until the vegetables are beginning to cook through but are still crisp.

Stir in the garlic and ginger paste and fry for about a minute. Add the tomato purée, mixed powder, chilli powder and about 250ml (1 cup) of the base curry sauce. This will come to an instant bubble. Add the chicken, stock and the rest of the base curry sauce.

Let this simmer over a medium heat for about 5 minutes, without stirring unless it is obviously catching on the pan. If the sauce begins to caramelize around the edges of the pan, stir this back into the curry. Add more base sauce or cooking stock if the sauce becomes too thick.

About 2 minutes before serving, add the quartered tomatoes and dried fenugreek (methi) leaves.

When the tomatoes are cooked through but still crisp and you are happy with the consistency, season with salt to taste and sprinkle with the garam masala. Finish by garnishing with the chopped coriander leaves and sliced chillies.

Now you get to put that pre-cooked keema (see page 28) to work. I've specified lamb keema here but any meat keema will do.

Whenever I make this curry, I usually also prepare a selection of different samosas the same day using the pre-cooked keema. Just take out what you need for the samosas and use the rest in the curry. I would like to stress how much magnificent additional flavour you get by pre-cooking the keema meat. Yes, you could just throw it in raw for this recipe, but you would be missing one of the flavour boosts that makes BIR dishes so amazing.

To make this dish even more exciting, try adding a few more complementary ingredients. Chickpeas, blended spinach, pre-cooked potatoes (see page 29) and/or tandoori prawns (page 100), for example, could be all that's needed to take this popular curry and make it into a personal masterpiece.

LAMB KEEMA
SERVES 4 OR MORE AS PART OF A MULTI-COURSE MEAL

3 tbsp rapeseed oil or seasoned oil (see p7)
½ onion, very finely chopped
¼ red pepper (bell pepper), deseeded and finely chopped
2 tbsp garlic and ginger paste (see p18)
2 fresh green bullet chillies, finely chopped
2 tbsp finely chopped coriander (cilantro) stalks
2 tbsp mixed powder (see p17)
1 tsp ground cumin
1 tsp chilli powder or to taste
125ml (½ cup) tomato purée (see p19)
500ml (2 cups) base curry sauce (see p22), heated
1 quantity pre-cooked keema (see p28)
150g (1 cup) frozen peas
1 tomatoes, cut into 8 wedges
1 tsp dried fenugreek (methi) leaves
1 tsp garam masala (see p14)
3 tbsp chopped coriander (cilantro) leaves
2 tbsp julienned ginger
Salt

Heat the oil in a pan over a medium-high heat until sizzling hot. Add the onion and pepper (bell pepper) and fry for about 2 minutes until the onion is soft and just beginning to brown. Add the garlic and ginger paste, chillies and coriander (cilantro) stalks, and move it all around in the pan so that everything is nicely coated in the oil.

Stir in the mixed powder, cumin and chilli powder, give it all a good stir and then add the tomato purée. Let this sizzle for about 30 seconds and then pour in about 250ml (1 cup) of the base curry sauce and let it bubble for about 30 seconds. There's no need to stir unless it is obviously catching on the pan. Stir in the pre-cooked keema and the rest of the base curry sauce. This is usually a dry curry, but if you prefer more sauce, go ahead and add it, or a little meat stock.

Add the peas, tomato and dried fenugreek leaves and cook for a further minute or two until the peas are heated through. Be careful not to overcook them; they need to be plump and still have a bit of a bite to them. Simmer them too long and they will turn wrinkly and rather unappetizing.

Add salt to taste and sprinkle with the garam masala, chopped coriander and julienned ginger to serve.

Good British lamb saag (saag gosht) is very close to the authentic Punjabi version. In the subcontinent, the meat is slowly cooked on the bone in a large karahi until the lamb almost falls off the bone into the rich spinach sauce. Some British Pakistani and Punjabi restaurants still prepare the curry in this way and promote it as one of their house special dishes.

At most curry houses, however, it's made in under 10 minutes using prepared ingredients and plenty of cooking stock from pre-cooked lamb. This recipe might be quick, but when done correctly, it will taste like it's been gently simmering for hours. If you like buttery ghee, this is a good one to use it in.

LAMB SAAG

SERVES 4 OR MORE AS PART OF A MULTI-COURSE MEAL

225g (½lb) baby spinach leaves
3–6 fresh green bullet chillies, to taste
Bunch of fresh coriander (cilantro), leaves only (reserve stalks, see below)
4 tbsp ghee, rapeseed oil or seasoned oil (see p7)
1 onion, finely chopped
2 tbsp garlic paste (see p18)
1 tbsp ginger paste (see p18)
3 tbsp finely chopped coriander (cilantro) stalks
1 tbsp ground cumin
1 tbsp ground coriander
1 tbsp mixed powder (see p17)
1 tsp chilli powder
180ml (¾ cup) tomato purée (see p19)
375ml (1½ cups) base curry sauce (see p22), heated
600g (1 lb 5 oz) pre-cooked stewed lamb (see p27), plus 250ml (1 cup) of its cooking stock
2 tbsp plain yoghurt
Juice of 1 lemon
1 tbsp garam masala (see p14)
Salt and freshly ground pepper

NOTE: I prefer to use more garlic than ginger in this recipe. You could use equally measured garlic and ginger paste.

Put the spinach, chillies and coriander (cilantro) leaves in a food processor and blend to a smooth paste with a little water (or spice stock, see p18). Set aside.

Heat the ghee or oil in a frying pan over a medium-high heat. When hot, add the onion and fry for about 5 minutes until translucent and soft but not overly browned. Add the garlic and ginger pastes, and allow to sizzle for about 30 seconds. Add the coriander stalks, ground cumin and coriander, mixed powder and chilli powder, and stir to combine.

Swirl in the tomato purée and about 250ml (1 cup) of the base curry sauce and let it come to a happy simmer. Add the stock and the rest of the base sauce. You can let it simmer for a few minutes and you don't need to stir unless it is obviously catching on the pan. Be sure to stir in any caramelized sauce from the sides of the pan from time to time.

Add the pre-cooked lamb pieces and simmer in the sauce until heated through. When the sauce is about the consistency you prefer, pour in the spinach purée and stir it all up. The bright green spinach will become darker as it cooks. Simmer for a further couple of minutes. If the sauce becomes too dry for your liking, just add a little more base sauce and/or lamb stock. To finish, season with salt and pepper to taste. Stir in the yoghurt 1 tbsp at a time then top with a squeeze of lemon juice and the garam masala.

OTHER IDEAS: To make this curry even more interesting, add more texture, such as chickpeas or pre-cooked potatoes (see p29).

Just like many of the British versions of Indian curries, our lamb rogan josh is quite a lot different to those made in India. Mutton or lamb rogan josh originates from the Kashmir region of India where it is made with tempered whole spices such as cloves, cinnamon, bay leaves, cardamom and deseeded Kashmiri dried chillies. Meat on the bone is braised in a sauce that is deep red in colour, both from the Kashmiri chillies and roton jot, which is a natural red food colouring and difficult to come by in the West, where the red colouring is achieved with paprika and tomato.

LAMB ROGAN JOSH
SERVES 4 OR MORE AS PART OF A MULTI-COURSE MEAL

4 tbsp rapeseed oil or seasoned oil (see p7)
2 tbsp garlic and ginger paste (see p18)
2 tbsp paprika
1 tsp chilli powder, or more to taste
125ml (½ cup) tomato purée (see p19)
500ml (2 cups) base curry sauce (see p22), heated
1 tbsp ground cumin
1½ tbsp mixed powder (see p17)
700g (1½ lb) pre-cooked stewed lamb (see p27), plus 200ml (scant 1 cup) of its cooking stock
2 tomatoes, quartered
2–3 tbsp raw cashew paste (see p19)
3 tbsp plain yoghurt
1 tsp dried fenugreek (methi) leaves
1 tsp garam masala (see p14)
3 tbsp chopped coriander (cilantro) leaves
Chopped red onion, to garnish
Salt

Heat the oil in a large frying pan over a medium-high heat until hot. Add the garlic and ginger paste and let it sizzle for about 30 seconds, stirring continuously. Add the paprika and chilli powder and fry for about 30 seconds. The mixture should turn a darker red as it cooks. Pour in the tomato purée, which should start to bubble as soon as it hits the pan. Cook it down by about half then stir in 250ml (1 cup) of the base curry sauce, the cumin and mixed powder.

Allow the sauce to simmer for a couple of minutes, without stirring unless it is obviously catching on the pan. Some of the sauce should caramelize to the sides of the pan; you want to scrape it off from time to time as it adds a nice smoky flavour. Add the pre-cooked lamb and the rest of the base sauce with the stock.

Let the sauce come to a boil until it reduces to your preferred consistency, only stirring if it is catching. Add the tomato wedges to the sauce.

To serve, swirl in the cashew paste then add the yoghurt 1 tbsp at a time, stirring continuously. Sprinkle with the dried fenugreek leaves, garam masala and add salt to taste. Top with the coriander (cilantro) and garnish with chopped red onion and a little plain yoghurt.

Authentic Indian bhunas are quite a lot more difficult to make than this British restaurant-style version. Bhuna is a style of cooking where hot oil or ghee is used to release the flavours of whole spices before raw meat is added, often as small pieces still on the bone.

Once the meat is added, stock or water is drizzled into the pan in small amounts, cooking the meat as it reduces down. This process is repeated for an hour or more until the meat becomes fall-off-the-bone tender and served in the thick sauce it was cooked in. This time-consuming style of cooking wouldn't be possible in most restaurants. This is still a dry curry, but made in a fraction of the time. Cooked boneless meat is used instead of braised raw meat.

LAMB BHUNA

SERVES 4 OR MORE AS PART OF A MULTI-COURSE MEAL

3 tbsp ghee, rapeseed oil or seasoned oil (see p7)
1 small onion, finely chopped
¼ red pepper (bell pepper), deseeded and roughly chopped
2 tbsp garlic and ginger paste (see p18)
2 tbsp finely chopped coriander (cilantro) stalks (from the bunch below)
125ml (½ cup) tomato purée (see p19)
2 tbsp mixed powder (see p17)
2 tbsp tandoori masala (see p15)
500ml (2 cups) base curry sauce (see p22), heated
800g (1¾lb) pre-cooked stewed lamb, plus 250ml (1 cup) of its cooking stock, or more base sauce
2 tbsp Greek yoghurt
Small bunch of coriander (cilantro), leaves finely chopped
Salt and freshly ground pepper
Juice of 1 or 2 limes
Sliced red chilli, to serve

Heat the ghee or oil in a large pan over a medium-high heat. When it is bubbling, add the onion and pepper (bell pepper) and sizzle them in the oil for about 5 minutes until the onion is translucent and soft. Stir in the garlic and ginger paste, and coriander (cilantro) stalks and stir these around in the oil for about 30 seconds.

Add the tomato purée and, when it starts to bubble, stir in the mixed powder and tandoori masala, followed by 250ml (1 cup) of the base curry sauce. Let this simmer for a couple of minutes, without stirring unless it is obviously catching on the pan. Scrape any caramelized sauce at the edges of the pan back in.

Increase the heat to high and add the pre-cooked lamb and the rest of the sauce, with the stock. Let this bubble undisturbed until it reduces down to a thick sauce.

To finish, reduce the heat to medium and whisk in the yoghurt 1 tbsp at a time. Check for seasoning and add salt and pepper to taste. Top with the fresh coriander and serve with a good squeeze of lime juice and/or some sliced red chilli, if you like.

Dining out with friends at a curry house right after I moved to the UK, I was told how to order from the menu by spice level. A simple lamb curry would be mild. A Madras would be the same but with more chilli powder. The vindaloo would have substantially more chilli powder and the phal, dangerously hot. That advice did me well back then, but nowadays the better chefs ensure each of these curries have a flavour all their own. It's not just down to the spiciness anymore.

I love this sweet-and-sour Madras. The addition of smooth mango chutney and a twist or two of lime juice makes this the perfect blend that can take centre stage at any curry feast.

LAMB MADRAS

SERVES 4 OR MORE AS PART OF A MULTI-COURSE MEAL

3 tbsp rapeseed oil or seasoned oil (see p7)

2–4 Kashmiri dried red chillies, to taste

A few green cardamom pods, lightly bruised

3 tbsp garlic and ginger paste (see p18)

2 fresh green chillies, or to taste, finely chopped

125ml (½ cup) tomato purée (see p19)

2 tbsp ground cumin

1 tsp ground coriander

¼ tsp ground turmeric

1–2 tbsp chilli powder, to taste

2 tbsp mixed powder (see p17)

500ml (2 cups) base curry sauce (see p22), heated

800g (1¾lb) pre-cooked stewed lamb (see p27), plus 250ml (1 cup) of its cooking stock, or more base curry sauce

1–2 tbsp smooth mango chutney, to taste

Juice of 1 lime

Pinch of garam masala (see p14)

Fresh coriander (cilantro), to garnish

Salt

Heat the oil in a pan over a medium-high heat until hot. Add the dried chillies and cardamom pods, and allow to sizzle for about 30 seconds. Be sure to count the cardamom pods in and count them back out again at the end of cooking if you don't like biting into whole spices. Scoop in the garlic and ginger paste along with the chopped chillies. Allow them to sizzle for about 20 seconds then stir in the tomato purée followed by the ground cumin, coriander and turmeric, the chilli powder and mixed powder.

Now add 250ml (1 cup) of the base curry sauce along with the lamb. Simmer for about 2 minutes, without stirring unless it is obviously catching on the pan, scraping back in any caramelized sauce from the sides of the pan. Pour in the rest of the base curry sauce and the stock, and let it simmer over a high heat until it has reduced down to your preferred consistency.

To serve, stir in the mango chutney and lime juice. Check for seasoning and add salt to taste. Sprinkle with the garam masala and garnish with the chopped coriander (cilantro).

TIP: If you are looking for a more savoury flavour, spicy lime pickle can be substituted for the mango chutney.

Many restaurants include potato in their vindaloo curries. Aloo means potato in Hindi so a lot of the original self-taught Bangladeshi and Pakistani chefs in the UK mistakenly added potatoes to this fiery curry, and it stuck. Vindaloo, however, owes its origins to Portuguese-controlled Goa in the 15th century, where the dish was usually served with pork. The name vindaloo was most likely a mispronunciation of the similar Portuguese dish *carne de vinho e alho* (meat with wine and garlic). So our vindaloo is completely different to the authentic Goan version other than it is quite spicy and often packs a vinegary punch. I don't add potatoes, but if you would like to, I've included instructions.

LAMB VINDALOO
SERVES 4 OR MORE AS PART OF A MULTI-COURSE MEAL

3 tbsp rapeseed oil or seasoned oil (see p7)
6 green cardamom pods, bashed
2 star anise
1 Indian bay leaf (cassia leaf)
2 tbsp garlic and ginger paste (see p18)
2 fresh green bullet chillies, finely chopped
2 Scotch bonnet chillies, finely chopped
1 tsp ground turmeric
2 tbsp hot chilli powder (be careful – if unsure, add less)
2 tbsp mixed powder (see p17)
125ml (½ cup) tomato purée (see p19)
2 tsp jaggery or sugar
600ml (2½ cups) base curry sauce (see p22), heated
800g (1¾lb) pre-cooked stewed lamb (see p27), plus 200ml (scant 1 cup) of its cooking stock
2 tbsp white wine vinegar
1 tsp dried fenugreek (methi) leaves
Approx. 2 pre-cooked stewed potatoes – about 8 pieces (see p29), (optional)
3 tbsp chopped coriander (cilantro)
Salt and freshly ground pepper

Heat the oil in a pan over a medium-high heat. When it begins to bubble, add the whole spices and bay leaf. If you don't like biting into whole spices, be sure to count them in and count them back out again before serving.

Scoop in the garlic and ginger paste and fry in the hot oil for about a minute. Add the chopped chillies, turmeric, chilli powder and mixed powder, followed by the tomato purée and jaggery or sugar. The tomato purée will bubble as it heat ups.

Pour in about 250ml (1 cup) of the base curry sauce and let it come to a rolling simmer. Don't stir the sauce unless it looks like it is beginning to catch. Scrape back in any sauce that caramelizes around the sides of the pan.

The pan should be going crazy over the heat. Swirl in the remaining base curry sauce and add the pre-cooked meat with a little of the cooking stock. Let the sauce simmer over the high heat until it cooks down to your desired consistency. Only stir it if it looks like it is catching on the pan.

To finish, add the vinegar, dried fenugreek leaves, potatoes if using, and the chopped coriander (cilantro). Check for seasoning and add salt and freshly ground pepper to taste.

BALTI, KARAHI AND HAANDI

I receive so many requests for balti, karahi and haandi recipes, mainly due to people having a favourite dish at their local Indian restaurant that includes one of these titles. The thing is, the reference to balti, karahi and haandi is not about the ingredients used but the style of pan in which the ingredients are supposedly cooked, as well as how they are cooked. I say supposedly because this isn't always the case.

I think it is a good idea here to explain what the differences are between the different pans, followed by a couple of recipes that are best cooked in them.

KARAHI PAN

An authentic karahi is a deep-sided, cast-iron pan used in Pakistan and other parts of the subcontinent for slow-cooking and stir-frying. It looks a lot like a wok with handles. Nowadays, they are also made of steel, aluminium and non-stick materials, but personally I think these don't compare to the original – and still most popular – heavy cast-iron pans. Karahis are available from small one-serving pans right up to pans that are large enough to prepare a curry for over fifty people.

HAANDI PAN

Haandi pans can be used in the same way as a karahi. They have a rounded, heavy base like a wok so that meat and vegetables can be cooked for long periods of time without catching on the base, just like a karahi. Haandis are different in shape to karahis in that they are narrow in the centre and then have a wide mouth at the top.

Some haandis have lids, making them perfect for steaming rice as well as slow-cooking amazing curries. They are manufactured in many different metals and also clay. Haandis, like karahis, are also available as large and more decorative small pans used in many curry houses for presentation.

BALTI PAN

Balti was invented in Birmingham. I know there are those who say that balti cooking comes from Baltistan or that balti pans are really only small karahis, but that simply isn't the case.

I spent a few days visiting Birmingham's Balti Triangle with my friend and respected balti historian Andy Munro. Andy grew up there in the 1950s, 60s and 70s, long before it was called the Balti Triangle – in fact, he claims he coined the now famous phrase for the area. Few people know balti like Andy.

There are many well-known Balti Triangle restaurateurs who were influential in the balti craze of the 1980s. Through Munro's meticulous research, however, he believes that one man is responsible for the balti-style pan and how baltis were – and in a few restaurants still are – served in the authentic style.

Mohammed Arif was the owner of long-established Adil's on Stoney Lane. He had substantial experience from several of Birmingham's Indian restaurants and knew how much 'Brummies' loved a good curry. In the late 1970s, Pakistani restaurants were attracting only the local Pakistani community, and Arif wanted to get the much larger population of Birmingham curry fans to Adil's.

One-pot cooking was popular in Pakistan as it made it possible to serve large groups of people. Slow-cooked curries would be prepared, usually with meat on the bone, and simmered in stock and spices until the meat was falling off the bone into the succulent sauce.

Arif wanted to bring this style of cooking to the greater population, but understood that most 'Western' curry fans wouldn't be prepared to wait an hour or longer to be served. He needed small single serving pans capable of heating up faster than cast-iron karahis.

At the time, the Birmingham area still had a substantial metal-bashing industry and Arif started searching for a company that could help him with his idea. He found Pressform, a company run by a Sikh by the name of Tara Singh. Arif asked if Singh could design a one-serving pan that looked like a karahi but was made out of thin, pressed steel, with a flat bottom rather than the rounded base of a karahi. This had the added benefit of heating up faster than cast iron. These balti pans had a mat-steel finish, which quickly turned their trademark black colour over the fierce heat of the flame.

Pressform is no longer in business, and with it went the only manufacturer of authentic British balti pans. There are copies made in India but restaurants complain that they are not the same quality. There are plans to have them manufactured once again in Birmingham.

The balti caught on fast in the early 1980s. It was new and fun. There was something pleasantly social about going out for a balti with friends and family, having the baltis served in the same intensely hot pans they were cooked in and then mopping it all up with a huge naan that was shared around the table.

So why is it called balti? There is a lot of speculation, but in Munro's opinion, after speaking with Arif and many other Balti Triangle restaurateurs, the answer is quite simple and believable. Pakistani restaurateurs at the time understood that chicken tikka masala and chicken biryani were the most common curries in British curry houses and the extent of most people's Indian cuisine vocabulary. They felt that describing the dish as a karahi was deceptive as it was not karahi-style cooking so much as the pan looked like a karahi. They also believed that the word karahi wasn't the catchiest or easiest word to pronounce. Balti in Hindi means bucket, and the word was already being used by many Pakistanis to describe a container that held food for weddings. Balti just seemed to slip off the tongue. It was catchy and, as we all now know, it caught on in a big way.

Almost any curry can be cooked as a balti. At Shababs, in Birmingham, they seem to have hundreds of combinations that can be ordered. The restaurant was packed when I visited with friend and balti historian Andy Munro. He commented that making baltis correctly was probably best left to the professionals, and after watching chef-owner Zafar Hussain cook a few, I could understand why. Don't let that stop you from making this one, though!

Authentic baltis are cooked over a high gas flame that is much hotter than is possible on most conventional hobs. As they are cooked, the whole pan turns into a big ball of fire as the oil catches light. You might think that this would burn the other ingredients but it doesn't. Only the oil is burned off, making the balti healthier and adding a delicious smoking flavour. When they place those sizzling hot curries in front of you, you know you're in for something special.

Cook it in a large one serving Balti pan just like at Shababs! A good frying pan can be substituted.

CHICKEN BALTI
SERVES 1

3 tbsp rapeseed oil or seasoned oil (see p7)
1 small onion, roughly chopped
1 green pepper (bell pepper), deseeded and roughly chopped
1 tomato, diced
1 tbsp garlic and ginger paste (see p18)
1 tbsp green chilli paste (see p18)
1 tsp ground cumin
1 tsp ground turmeric
1 tsp paprika
250ml (1 cup) base curry sauce (see p22), heated
200g (7oz) skinless chicken breast or thigh meat, cut into small pieces (tikka)
1 tbsp garam masala (see p14)
1 tsp dried fenugreek (methi) leaves
Salt
Chopped coriander (cilantro), to serve

Heat the oil in a frying pan (or wok, karahi or balti pan) over a high heat until almost smoking. Add the onion, pepper (bell pepper) and tomato, and fry for about a minute. Stir in the garlic and ginger paste and chilli paste. The oil will sizzle as they release their moisture.

If you're feeling brave and have a gas hob, tilt the pan towards the flame and see if you can get the oil to catch fire. Don't panic if it lights, and never throw water on the flame or you will probably have to call the fire service and may need a new kitchen.

Add the ground spices and 5 tbsp of the base curry sauce. Let this come to a boil then add the chicken pieces and another 5 tbsp of the base sauce. Stir occasionally so that the sauce doesn't catch, and scrape the caramelized sauce from the sides of the pan.

Pour in the remaining base sauce and let the curry simmer until the chicken is cooked through and the sauce is quite thick. Baltis are usually served with fresh naans or chapatis, which are used to soak up the sauce and meat instead of cutlery, and your sauce needs to be thick enough to do this.

To finish, stir in the garam masala and dried fenugreek leaves and check for seasoning. If there is any oil on the surface, skim it off for a healthier curry. Top with chopped coriander (cilantro) to serve.

I got to watch this curry being prepared at Imran's in Birmingham by head chef, Talib Hussain. It was drop-dead gorgeous and I've made it many times since. At Imran's, the meat is cut into small pieces still on the bone. Boneless lamb can be substituted, but personally I like it their way. It may be a bit messier to eat, but dipping your naan into this delicious sauce and trying to gnaw every last bit of meat off the bone is part of the experience.

Owner and executive chef Usman Butt said he would normally prepare such a dish in a karahi. On their menu, chef Talib calls it a haandi. Whichever you use, you are going to love this one.

LAMB KARAHI
SERVES 4 OR MORE AS PART OF A MULTI-COURSE MEAL

800g (1¾lb) lamb leg and shoulder, cut into pieces, ideally still with bone in

FOR THE MARINADE
1 tbsp rapeseed oil
100g (½ cup) Greek yoghurt
2 tbsp garlic and ginger paste (see p18)
1 tsp salt
1 tbsp freshly ground black pepper

FOR THE SAUCE
4 tbsp rapeseed oil
2 tbsp garlic and ginger paste (see p18)
1 quantity fried onions (see p19)
1 tbsp pungent dried red chilli flakes
2 large tomatoes, diced
1½ tbsp ground cumin
1½ tbsp ground coriander
1 tbsp Kashmiri chilli powder
3 tbsp julienned ginger
2 fresh green bullet chillies, roughly chopped
1 tsp garam masala (see p14)
Fresh coriander (cilantro), to serve

Mix the meat pieces with the marinade ingredients in a large bowl and cover with cling film (plastic wrap). Leave to marinate in the fridge for at least 2 hours, or ideally overnight; the longer the better.

When ready to cook, heat the oil in a pan over a medium-high heat and add the garlic and ginger paste. Stir this around for about 30 seconds then add the meat and all the marinade. Using a large spoon, stir to coat the meat with the garlicky oil. Add the fried onions, chilli flakes and tomatoes and again stir it all up to combine.

Now sprinkle in the ground cumin, coriander and chilli powder. Pour in just enough water to cover and let it all simmer for a good 40 minutes to 1 hour. You may need to top up the water from time to time.

Check for seasoning and add more salt or spices to taste. This is a quite dry curry so that it can easily be soaked up with fresh naans. When the meat is really tender, add the julienned ginger, fresh chillies and garam masala and serve topped with fresh coriander (cilantro).

That's it! This may be simple, but believe me no one will know. Serve it to friends and they'll think you've been secretly working as the head chef of Imran's!

GRILLING, BARBECUE AND ROASTING

In this chapter I'm going to show you how to make some of my favourite tandoori dishes. Given the word tandoori, it would be fair to assume that everything is cooked in a tandoor oven, but this isn't always the case. Almost every Indian restaurant now has a tandoor oven but many, especially Pakistani-run operations, only use the tandoor for naans and parathas.

Some of the best 'tandoori' dishes I've had were actually cooked on skewers or on a grill over an open flame. I have a home tandoor oven, but I also usually only use it for naans. This is especially so when we're having a group of friends round. Cooking the meat, seafood, paneer and vegetables over the intense heat of the flames and the naans in the tandoor means that all the food can be served hot, at the same time.

Don't get me wrong. I do cook meat often in the tandoor for my family, and I do recommend getting one. Small home tandoor ovens cost about the same as a good gas barbecue, and get superior results. They reach temperatures near 400°C/750°F, which is how the meat and seafood gets so nicely charred and succulent.

These recipes use both indirect and direct grilling methods, and I have explained both. I've also given instructions for conventional ovens as well as tandoor cooking, just in case you're tempted.

PREPARING YOUR BARBECUE FOR DIRECT HEAT GRILLING

Cooking over open flames is the simplest of the three methods used. When your food is exposed to the intense direct heat, it gets a wonderful, smoky char on the exterior, while the interior remains deliciously juicy.

When preparing your charcoal, it is a good idea to build a two-level fire. Pour your charcoal into the basin of your barbecue. Then spread the charcoal so that two thirds of the coals are stacked about twice as high as the remaining one third. This way, you can easily move whatever it is you are cooking from the hot side of the grill to the cooler side if it begins to burn before it's cooked through.

I use a lot of charcoal – about two full shoe boxes* – as it is important to achieve that intense heat. Light your charcoal and let it heat up until your coals are white-hot. To check if the coals are ready, hold your hand about 5cm (2 in) above the fire. If your hand becomes uncomfortably hot in 2 seconds, you're ready start cooking.

I like to cook using flat skewers when cooking this way. Skewering meat, seafood, paneer and vegetables gives the finished dish that authentic tandoori-restaurant look. You could also use a grill (broiler).

PREPARING YOU BARBECUE FOR INDIRECT COOKING

This method is used for roasting and you will need a barbecue that has a tight-fitting lid. Fill your barbecue on one side only with about two shoe boxes full of charcoal*, leaving the other half empty. Light a few fire lighters and pile in the charcoal. Let it heat until white hot, then place the grill on top and whatever it is you are cooking over the side with no coals. Cover and cook. If you are barbecuing for a long period of time, you will need to throw a few handfuls of charcoal on the fire every half hour or so.

PREPARING YOUR HOME TANDOOR OVEN FOR COOKING

Open the bottom vent completely and place a few fire lighters in the tandoor opposite the vent. Pour in about two shoe boxes full of charcoal and light, ensuring that you strategically stack as many pieces of charcoal as you can over the flames. It is important that your charcoal is as far away from the vent as possible so that air can flow freely.

Once the fire is burning nicely, place the lid on, leaving a crack open so that air can flow from the vent to the top. Close the bottom vent so that it is only one-third open. You can now relax with a beer or two for about an hour while it heats up. To work properly, the clay walls of the oven need to be extremely hot and the tandoor needs to be at least 230°C/450°F.

If you are cooking with a tandoor for the first time, be sure to read the manual first, and cure the clay walls before cooking anything.

OVEN COOKING

Ovens vary but I usually crank mine up to 200°C/400°F/gas mark 6 and cook the meat on a wire rack near the top. To get that charred appearance and flavour, place the roasted meat under a hot grill for a couple of minutes after cooking, before serving.

*The amount of charcoal you use depends on the size of your barbecue. Refer to your owner's manual for the manufacturer's recommendations. The Thüros Kebab Grill, shown in many of the photos in this section, requires a lot less than larger kettle barbecues.

This is a tasty way of serving these vegetables. They can be served as a side dish or you could add the vegetables to any curries in this book to make a vegetarian version. The gram (chickpea) flour adds flavour and makes the marinade thicker, which is really nice grilled.

You could also place the vegetables on a lightly oiled baking tray and cook them in a hot oven until lightly charred and cooked through.

TANDOORI BROCCOLI, CAULIFLOWER AND RED ONION

SERVES 4 OR MORE AS PART OF A MULTI-COURSE MEAL

1 head of broccoli, separated into bite-sized florets
1 head of cauliflower, separated into bite-sized florets
1 red onion, quartered and divided into individual petals
3 tbsp gram (chickpea) flour
2 tbsp plain yoghurt
1 tbsp rapeseed oil
1 tbsp garam masala (see p14)
1 tsp chilli powder
Pinch of ground turmeric
Juice of 1 lemon
Salt

Bring a pan of water to a boil and add the broccoli and cauliflower florets. Boil for 2–3 minutes to par-cook them. Drain and leave to cool.

Put the cooled vegetables in a large bowl with the onion. Mix together the chickpea (gram) flour, yoghurt, oil, garam masala, chilli powder, turmeric and lemon juice, and pour over the vegetables. Stir so that all of the vegetables are equally coated.

When ready to cook, prepare your barbecue for direct heat grilling (see page 88). Thread the vegetables onto skewers and cook directly over the hot coals until cooked through and charred.

Season with salt and serve immediately.

These are excellent served outside, straight off the barbecue. You can prepare them indoors up to the end of the frying stage, then take them outside and cook over indirect heat (see page 88) on the barbecue. Like all of the tandoori recipes in this book, you can also cook them in the oven, as I have here.

Cook the hard-boiled eggs to your liking. For soft yolks, boil the eggs for no more than 7 minutes, and for hard yolks 10–12 minutes. The meat is prepared exactly as the lamb seekh kebab recipe on page 96.

This is a great recipe for parties as most of the work can be done ahead of time. Even the frying can be done a good hour before guests arrive, so all you need to do is heat them up in the oven or on the barbecue.

NARGISI KOFTA (INDIAN SCOTCH EGG)
MAKE 1 KOFTA PER PERSON

150g (5½ oz) seekh kebab minced lamb (see p96) per egg
Hard-boiled eggs, 1 per person (see cooking times above), peeled
Chickpea (gram) flour, for dusting
1 egg, beaten
Toasted breadcrumbs, for coating
Vegetable oil, for frying

For each egg, roll out 150g (5½ oz) minced lamb mixture between two layers of cling film (plastic wrap), so that it is about 5mm (¼ in) thick, and flat. Remove the top layer of cling film and place a hard-boiled egg in the middle. Using the bottom sheet of cling film, bring the meat up and form it around the egg.

Dust in the chickpea (gram) flour then coat in the beaten egg and roll in the breadcrumbs until fully coated. (This work can all be done ahead of time for ease. Just place the coated koftas on a plate, cover with cling film and store in the fridge.)

When ready to cook, pour about a 5cm (2in) depth of oil into a wok and heat over a high heat. When a few breadcrumbs sizzle immediately when thrown in, it is ready. Lower a nargisi kofta into the oil and fry all over for about 3 minutes until nicely browned. Remove with a slotted spoon to a plate lined with kitchen paper, and repeat until all the koftas are fried.

To finish, preheat the oven to 200°C/400°F/gas mark 6 or prepare your barbecue for indirect cooking (see page 88). If refrigerated, remove the koftas from the fridge to come to room temperature. Place the fried koftas on a baking tray and roast in the oven or barbecue for about 7 minutes – the meat should already be cooked from the frying, so the oven or barbecue roasting will just warm them through.

Red food colouring powder is often added to chicken tikka to give it the appearance of being spicy hot. I often add red food colouring to my chicken tikka but it doesn't add any flavour and can be left out. Beetroot powder is often used as a substitute but it doesn't achieve that bright red curry-house look.

This recipe is amazing on its own but you could also use it in curries such as chicken tikka masala and chicken chilli garlic (see pages 53 and 63). I usually cook these chicken pieces (tikka) on skewers over a hot charcoal fire, but you could also cook them on a rack in the oven at about 200°C/400°F/gas mark 6. See photograph on page 94.

TANDOORI CHICKEN TIKKA
SERVES 4 OR MORE AS PART OF A MULTI-COURSE MEAL

1kg (2¼ lb) skinless, boneless chicken breasts, cut into bite-sized pieces (tikka)
Juice of 2 lemons
3 tbsp garlic and ginger paste (see p18)
Red food colouring powder (optional)
Salt

FOR THE MARINADE
210g (1 cup) Greek yoghurt, whisked
1 tbsp ground cumin
1 tbsp ground coriander
1 tbsp garam masala (see p14)
1 tbsp tandoori masala (see p15)
1 tsp amchoor (dried mango powder)
1 tsp ground turmeric
1 tsp paprika or chilli powder
2 fresh green chillies, finely chopped or green chilli paste (see p18)
3 tbsp finely grated Parmesan cheese
20g coriander (cilantro) leaves, finely chopped
1 tsp salt
1 tbsp freshly ground black pepper

Place the chicken pieces (tikka) in a large bowl, squeeze the lemon juice over them and sprinkle with a little salt. Stir in the garlic and ginger paste and some red food colouring, if you want the authentic chicken tikka colour. Mix it all up really well and set aside while you make the marinade.

Place the marinade ingredients in a bowl and mix with your hands until good and smooth. Cover the chicken pieces with the marinade, ensuring they are completely coated. Cover and marinate in the fridge for at least 6 hours or up to 48 hours; the longer the better.

When ready to cook, prepare your barbecue for direct cooking (see page 88). When your coals are white hot, thread the chicken tikka onto skewers and place over the coals, turning occasionally until the chicken is cooked through and the edges are blackened. You can also do this on a grill.

Season with salt to taste and serve hot, or use in your curries.

TIPS
★When grilling skewered chicken, the raw pieces will move around a lot when turned. I suggest leaving to cook through on one side before turning. The meat will expand as it cooks and you will not experience as much annoying movement on the skewers.
★Try to leave a little space between each piece of chicken on the skewer so that it cooks evenly. For better presentation, you could move the meat chunks closer together, once cooked through, if serving on the skewers.

I've learned so much from my friend Chef Palash Mitra over the past few years. This recipe is one I simply had to share with you. The tender chunks of chicken are awesome served on their own with a tasty raita. It is equally as good added to a curry, such as the butter chicken (see page 132).

Before I watched Palash prepare this marinade, I used to simply throw my marinades together in a couple of minutes. Palash took his time and blended the ingredients together by hand into a smooth emulsion. It is obvious he loves what he does, and his meticulous style and attention to detail really do make a big difference. See photograph on page 94.

TANDOORI MURGH MALAI TIKKA
SERVES 4 OR MORE AS PART OF A MULTI-COURSE MEAL

5 tbsp rapeseed oil
2 tbsp garlic and ginger paste (see p18)
1½ tsp salt
1½ tsp ground turmeric
2–4 green bird's-eye chillies, finely chopped
2 tsp lemon juice
Pinch of saffron threads
1kg (2¼ lb) skinless chicken thighs, boned and diced
250ml (1 cup) double (heavy) cream
2 tbsp ghee
2 tsp royal (black) cumin seeds
3 tbsp cream cheese
4 tbsp finely chopped fresh coriander (cilantro)
100g (½ cup) Greek yoghurt

Pour the oil into a deep tray and add the garlic and ginger paste, salt, turmeric, chopped chillies, lemon juice and saffron. Add the chicken pieces and half the cream. Rub this into the chicken, cover and marinate overnight in the fridge.

The next day, heat the ghee in a small pan over a low heat, add the royal (black) cumin seeds and let them splutter. Cool the ghee to room temperature, pour it over the chicken, cold from the fridge and mix well.

Push the chicken with its marinade to one side of the tray and spoon in the rest of the cream, the cream cheese, chopped coriander (cilantro) and yoghurt to the other side of the tray.

Work these ingredients together with your hands until they are completely emulsified. This takes about 5 minutes. Mix into the chicken, cover and marinate in the fridge for 24 hours.

To cook the chicken, thread the pieces onto skewers and grill, using the direct heat method (see page 88) until lightly charred on the underside. Flip over the chicken skewers and grill the other side until cooked through. Alternately, bake in an oven at 200°C/400°F/gas mark 6 for 6–8 minutes or until cooked through.

NOTE: Palash adds 1 tsp of sandlewood powder to his marinade. It isn't easy to find but if you come across some, give it a go!

The soola marinade in this recipe is popular not just for chicken but red meat and vegetables too. Red meat such as venison, beef and lamb can be marinated for three days and the end result is so good. With chicken, duck and other poultry and feathered game, I usually marinate the meat for 24–48 hours. Seafood only needs about 20 minutes.

For me, mustard oil is a must with this recipe. You could substitute rapeseed oil but you will get a different flavour. Please read my note on mustard oil on page 155.

CHICKEN SOOLA KEBABS
SERVES 4 OR MORE AS PART OF A MULTI-COURSE MEAL

1 tbsp cloves
Seeds from 6 black
    cardamom pods
2 tbsp black peppercorns
1 tbsp fennel seeds
1 tbsp cumin seeds
1 tbsp coriander seeds
3 tbsp ghee
2 tbsp mustard oil
1 large onion, finely chopped
8 garlic cloves, finely chopped
2 large bunches of coriander
    (cilantro), leaves only
100g (½ cup) plain yoghurt
8 skinless, boneless chicken
    breasts, cut into bite-sized
    pieces (tikka)
Juice of 2 limes
1 tsp chaat masala (see p14)
Salt and freshly ground pepper

Heat a frying pan over a medium heat. Throw in the cloves, cardamom seeds, peppercorns, and the fennel, cumin and coriander seeds, and move them around in the pan so that they roast evenly. When they become warm and fragrant, tip onto a plate, allow to cool a little, then grind them into a powder using a spice grinder or pestle and mortar.

Heat the ghee and mustard oil together in the frying pan. Add the onion and fry until translucent and soft, but not browned. Add the garlic and fry for a further minute, then remove from the heat and allow to cool.

Transfer to a food processor with the ground spices, coriander (cilantro) leaves and 1 tsp salt, and blend until smooth. Transfer to a bowl, add the yoghurt and whisk together. Add the chicken pieces and stir to coat, then cover and marinate in the fridge for at least 3 hours or up to 48 hours; the longer the better.

When ready to cook, light your barbecue using the direct cooking method (see page 88). Thread the chicken pieces onto skewers and cook, turning them until nicely charred on the exterior and cooked through. Transfer to a warm plate and squeeze the lime juice over the top. Sprinkle with the chaat masala and season with salt and pepper to taste.

I like to serve this with a simple green salad and coriander, garlic and chilli raita.

How can you not love a good, grilled lamb seekh kebab? They're great on their own, simply dipped into a spicy raita or two and even more delicious wrapped into a homemade naan with lots of crispy cold salad. I've tried more complicated recipes but this is my 'go to' recipe. Use the best quality minced meat you can find and the rest of the ingredients will bring out its natural flavour to perfection.

Texture is important! If you have a good butcher, ask him or her to run the meat through their grinder three or four times. You can also achieve this texture at home with the method I describe below. It's what my friend Hasan Chaudhry calls 'lacing' and it really makes these kebabs special.

LAMB SEEKH KEBABS
SERVES 4 OR MORE AS PART OF A MULTI-COURSE MEAL

1kg (2¼ lb) lean minced lamb
1 egg
2 tbsp green chilli paste
   (see p18)
2 onions, finely chopped
1 tbsp freshly roasted ground
   coriander (see p12)
1 tbsp garam masala (see p14)
Large bunch of coriander
   (cilantro), finely chopped
1 tsp salt

Place the lamb mince in a large bowl. Mix in the remaining ingredients and begin kneading the mixture with your hands. When all the ingredients are nicely mixed, begin pressing down on the meat, scraping it against the bottom of the bowl. The meat should streak against the bottom of the bowl, giving a 'lace' texture (see above), which will take about 5 minutes of kneading.

Form the mixture into meatballs the size of tennis balls. Slide a meatball onto a large, flat skewer and squeeze with a wet hand into a sausage shape around the skewer. Turn the skewer over and do the same, squeezing again with your hand to make it longer. Continue this process until you have a long kebab with visible finger marks that is securely on the skewer. Repeat with the rest of the meat mixture.

Heat your barbecue using the direct heat method (see page 88) then place the kebabs over the heat. Char well on one side then flip them over and do the same on the other side. When nicely blackened and cooked through, serve with salad, raita and/or chutney (they are especially good with the mint, coriander and mango chutney on page 141). These are delicious served wrapped up in hot homemade naans. You could also pan-fry the kebabs, but I tend not to. It just isn't the same.

ALTERNATIVE MEAT MIXTURE: To make an eggless version of these kebabs, mix 800g (1¾ lb) minced lamb with 200g (7 oz) minced chicken. The chicken is stickier than the lamb and helps keep the meat on the skewer just as the egg does.

If you love lobster like I do, nothing more needs to be said. Just look at it! You will need a sharp pair of kitchen scissors.

TANDOORI LOBSTER
SERVES 2

FOR THE LOBSTER STOCK
2 tbsp butter
Retained cracked claw shells
  with remaining meat
½ onion – finely chopped
2 Indian bay leaves
  (cassia leaves)
250ml (1 cup) dry white wine

FOR THE LOBSTERS
2 x 750g (1¾ lb) live lobsters
2 tbsp ghee
1 tsp brown mustard seeds
20 fresh or frozen curry leaves
½ onion, very finely chopped
1 tbsp garlic paste (see p18)
1 tsp ground cumin
1 tsp chilli powder
1 tsp English mustard
2 tbsp plain yoghurt
150ml (scant ⅔ cup) double
  (heavy) cream
Pinch of saffron threads
  (optional)
4 tbsp grated Parmesan cheese
3 tbsp finely chopped
  coriander (cilantro)
Juice of 2 limes or lemons
Salt

*Sedate the lobsters for 1 hour in the freezer before cooking. Transfer the lobsters from the freezer to a cutting board and firmly insert the tip of a sharp chef's knife into the cross on the back of the head, with the blade facing forward, and bring it down, slicing the head in half.

Cook your lobsters in a large pot of salty boiling water for no more than 4 minutes. Remove to cool. Remove the top of the shells from the tail and body with your scissors. Twist off the claws. Transfer the tail meat to a clean bowl and remove and discard the black and green innards in the body. Place the hollowed shells on a baking tray, cover and place them and the tail meat in the fridge.

Now crack open the claw shells (messy job) and remove the meat from inside to another clean bowl. The small amount of meat you can't get at easily will help flavour the stock.

To make the stock, melt the butter in a large saucepan over a medium heat and add the retained cracked lobster claw shells. Stir the shells around in the hot butter for about 10 minutes, then add the onion and bay leaves. Pour in the wine and just enough water to cover. Simmer for about 20 minutes, then strain through a sieve into a clean bowl.

Preheat your oven to its highest setting or prepare your barbecue for indirect cooking (see page 88).

Melt the ghee in a pan over a high heat until bubbly hot and add the mustard seeds. When they begin to pop, turn down the heat to medium and add the curry leaves. Add the onion and fry for about 10 minutes until translucent and soft but not browned. Now add the garlic paste, cumin, chilli powder and mustard, and stir to combine.

Pour in 150ml (scant ⅔ cup) of the lobster stock and turn up the heat to bring the mixture to a boil. Reduce this sauce by half, then whisk in the yoghurt, cream and saffron. Simmer for another 5–10 minutes to thicken. Check for seasoning, add salt to taste and set aside to cool slightly.

Pour the warm sauce over each bowl of lobster meat and spoon the mixture back into the shells. I usually place the meat from the two claws in the body and the tail meat in the tails. You may not be able to use all the sauce. Sprinkle with the Parmesan and transfer to the oven or barbecue for 4–5 minutes, until the meat is just cooked through and hot. Watch closely so you don't overcook!

Transfer each to a hot plate, garnish with coriander and serve with lemon or lime wedges.

These prawns (shrimp) are addictive. They are superb served on their own, dipped into a tasty raita, or added to a curry. That said, I think they are much too good to be thrown in a curry. I like to serve them drizzled with my honey mustard raita (see page 145) that goes so well with most seafood.

This is another recipe from my friend Chef Palash Mitra. One of the spice blends Palash recommends in the recipe is mace and ground cardamom powder, which is so simple to make: just grind equal amounts of mace and green cardamom seeds together into a powder. This delicate spice blend adds a subtle flavour that takes the tandoori prawns to a whole new level.

TANDOORI-STYLE KING PRAWNS
SERVES 4 OR MORE AS PART OF A MULTI-COURSE MEAL

500g (1 lb 2 oz) raw king prawns (jumbo shrimp), peeled and de-veined with head and tail intact

FOR THE FIRST MARINADE
1 tbsp rapeseed oil
2 tsp garlic and ginger paste (see p18)
¼ tsp ground turmeric
1 tsp salt
½ tsp finely ground white pepper

FOR THE SECOND MARINADE
2 tbsp Greek yoghurt
1 tbsp cream cheese
1 tbsp single (light) cream
1cm (½ in) piece of ginger, peeled and finely chopped
1 fresh green chilli, finely chopped
1 tbsp chopped fresh coriander (cilantro)
1 tsp macc and cardamom powder (see above)
1 tsp salt
1 tsp garlic powder
1 tsp ajwain (carom) seeds

Prepare your barbecue for direct heat cooking (see page 88).

Mix the prawns (shrimp) with the ingredients for the first marinade and set aside. Combine all the ingredients for the second marinade and work them together with your hands until you have a smooth emulsion. Cover the prawns with this marinade and leave for about 20 minutes.

Thread the prawns onto skewers and place over the hot fire. (You can also cook them directly on a barbecue grill.) Cook, turning frequently, until lightly charred and cooked through.

I must make this recipe once a week in the summer. You only need to throw it on the barbecue for a few minutes and, voilà, you've got yourself a dinner that not only tastes great but looks amazing. My fishmonger gets wild sea bass and bream for me, which is a lot better than the farmed stuff. It's a little more expensive, but when you're making a fancy meal like this it's worth every penny.

TANDOORI WHOLE FISH
SERVES 2

2 whole bream or sea bass, cleaned
1 tbsp garlic and ginger paste (see p18)
4 tbsp white wine vinegar
1 tsp rapeseed oil
1 tsp chilli powder
2 tbsp tandoori masala (see p15)
1 tsp garam masala (see p14)
1½ tbsp plain yoghurt
1 lemon, quartered
Salt

Make shallow slits on each side of the fish. Put the garlic and ginger paste, vinegar, oil, chilli powder, tandoori masala, garam masala and yoghurt in a bowl and whisk into a marinade. Season with salt to taste then rub the marinade all over the fish, inside and out, and leave to marinate for about 30 minutes.

Meanwhile, prepare your barbecue for direct grilling (see page 88). Remove the fish from the marinade and place in a metal grill fish basket, or thread a couple of skewers through to hold it in place. Cook, turning regularly, until the skin is nicely charred and the fish is cooked through. Serve with a squeeze of lemon.

This is a really nice way to grill salmon. The marinade is sweet and garlicky, and as you only grill the salmon for about 5 minutes, it is nicely charred on the exterior and so succulent. I prefer my salmon to be pink on the inside, but if you prefer yours to be completely cooked through, a couple more minutes over the coals will do the job.

You only need to marinate seafood for about 20 minutes. It soaks it all up. Don't marinate for longer than about 30 minutes or the lime juice will begin to 'cook' the fish and it will become tough.

Be sure to get thick-cut salmon fillets. If you can source wild salmon from your fishmonger, do it. You'll be glad you did.

TANDOORI SALMON
SERVES 4 OR MORE AS PART OF A MULTI-COURSE MEAL

1 tbsp finely grated lime zest
Juice of 2 limes
3 tbsp finely chopped fresh coriander (cilantro)
2 tbsp garlic and ginger paste (see p18)
1 tbsp finely chopped or pounded green chilli
1 tsp coarsely ground black pepper
5 tbsp light soy sauce
4 tbsp soft dark brown sugar
4 tbsp water
4 tbsp rapeseed oil
800g (1¾ lb) thick-cut salmon fillet, skinned and cut into bite-sized cubes

When ready to cook, fire up your barbecue for direct heat cooking (see page 88).

Place all the ingredients, except the salmon, in a large bowl and whisk together. Add the salmon cubes to the marinade and let them soak up the juices for 20 minutes.

Thread the salmon pieces onto flat skewers and cook over the coals for about 5 minutes (longer if you want the salmon cooked right through), turning regularly so that it takes on that amazing and tasty char, with a slight blackening on the outside.

Serve hot, simply with a green salad and nothing else. There is plenty of salt in the soy sauce, so I rarely add more.

These spicy paneer kebabs are a real treat, with a crispy, charred crust on the exterior and a deliciously soft centre. The kebabs are great served on their own or wrapped into hot homemade naans with the raita of your choice.

If you're working ahead of time, you can marinate these early in the day and then simply skewer them up and grill just before serving. See photograph on page 106.

PANEER SHASHLIK
SERVES 4 OR MORE AS PART OF A MULTI-COURSE MEAL

2 tbsp Greek yoghurt
1 tbsp garlic and ginger paste (see p18)
1 tsp chilli powder
1 tsp ground cumin
1 tsp ground coriander
1 tsp mixed powder (see p17)
1 tsp chaat masala (see p14)
½ tsp amchoor (dried mango powder)
1 tbsp vegetable oil
Juice of 1 lemon
1 large red pepper (bell pepper), deseeded and cut into pieces
1 medium red onion, cut into pieces
300g (10½ oz) paneer (see p30 for homemade), cubed

Put the yoghurt, garlic and ginger paste, spices, amchoor, oil and lemon juice in a bowl and mix together by hand. Add the pepper (bell pepper), onion and paneer to the marinade, stir to coat and leave to marinate for about 2 hours, or overnight in the fridge.

When ready to cook, light your barbecue using the direct grilling method (see page 88). Thread the vegetables and paneer onto skewers and grill over direct heat for 8–10 minutes, turning regularly until the middle of the paneer is hot and soft.

You can serve these as they are, on a plate, or wrap a naan around the skewer and pull the hot paneer and vegetables off into the naan. Top with your favourite raita or hot sauce.

I was invited to the Radisson Blu Edwardian at Heathrow a few years back to try their new restaurant Annayu and write a review on my blog. The head chef at the time, Madhup Sinha, really went to town trying to impress, and impress he did. He has since moved on to become head chef of Global Street Food Kitchen and has been such a valuable source of information, both with recipes and techniques.

The evening of my visit, Madhup prepared about 15 different dishes for me. I didn't eat for two days after that! They were all spectacular, but this one really caught my eye; it was beautiful. I didn't want to ruin it by cutting into it, but of course I did.

The good news is, it isn't difficult to make but don't tell anyone. Your guests will think you are some kind of master chef when you place this one in front of them.

TANDOORI PANEER CHUKANDARI

SERVES 4 OR MORE AS PART OF A MULTI-COURSE MEAL

2kg (4½ lb) raw beetroot (beet), peeled
1 tsp fine sea salt
1 tsp ajwain (carom) seeds
1 tsp royal (black) cumin seeds
2 tbsp ground white pepper
1½ tbsp garlic powder
5 tbsp garam masala (see p14)
700g (1½ lb) paneer (see p30 for homemade), cut into 7.5cm (3 in) cubes or slices 1cm (½ in) thick
350ml (1½ cups) balsamic vinegar
1½ tsp dried fenugreek (methi) leaves
1 tbsp tamarind concentrate
Sea salt
Chaat masala (see p14), to serve

Sprinkle the beetroot (beet) with sea salt and wrap in foil. Roast in the oven for about 45 minutes or until the beetroot is very soft, like potatoes cooked for mash. Weigh out 1.5kg (3 lb 5 oz) cooled beetroot (reserve the rest) and blend to a smooth paste in a food processor. In a bowl, stir the ajwain and cumin seeds, white pepper, garlic powder and garam masala into the beetroot paste.

Now add the paneer pieces and check for seasoning, adding a little more salt if needed. Stir gently to coat the paneer, cover and marinate in the fridge for 4 hours, or overnight.

Put the reserved roasted beetroot through a juicer if you have one. If not, blend it and pass it through a fine sieve a few times to obtain the juice. Add the balsamic vinegar to the beetroot juice, tip into a pan and reduce by half over a medium heat; keep warm (or reheat gently when ready to serve).

When ready to cook, preheat the oven to 180°C/350F°/gas mark 4 or set up your barbecue for indirect cooking (see page 88). Stir the dried fenugreek leaves and tamarind pulp into the marinade, then remove the paneer and spread out in a single layer in a roasting tin if roasting in the oven, or place on a rack to barbecue. Roast or barbecue until the paneer feels soft, 5–10 minutes.

Immediately drizzle the hot beetroot and vinegar reduction over the paneer, sprinkle with some chaat masala and serve.

POPULAR VEGETABLE AND SIDE DISHES

Any seasonal vegetables can be used for this recipe. I've recommended a few, but feel free to add whatever you like. Vegetable bhaji is essentially a stir-fry with a little base curry sauce and spices mixed in. Be careful not to over-cook the vegetables in the sauce. They need to have a bit of bite to them.

Consider this a slightly fancier version of the pre-cooked onions and vegetables on page 33. Vegetable bhaji can be served as a curry on its own, or you could mix a few spoonfuls into the curry of your choice.

VEGETABLE BHAJI
SERVES 4 OR MORE AS PART OF A MULTI-COURSE MEAL

2 tbsp rapeseed oil or
   seasoned oil (see p7)
1 tsp mustard seeds
10 fresh or frozen curry leaves
2 onions, thinly sliced
1 yellow and 1 red pepper
   (bell pepper), thinly sliced
2 tbsp garlic and ginger paste
   (see p18)
2 green bird's-eye chillies,
   finely chopped
½ tsp ground turmeric
2 tbsp Kashmiri paste (see p15)
   or mixed powder (see p17)
125ml (½ cup) tomato purée
   (see p19)
1 small carrot, peeled
   and thinly sliced
10 button mushrooms
20 green beans, cut into
   2.5cm (1 in) pieces
1 handful shredded cabbage
1 tbsp dried fenugreek
   (methi) leaves
400ml (1½ cups) base
   curry sauce (see p22)
1 tomato, quartered
Salt and freshly ground pepper
1 tbsp garam masala (see p14)

Heat the oil in a large wok or frying pan over a high heat. When hot, throw in the mustard seeds. When they begin to crackle, reduce the heat to medium-high, then add the curry leaves and stir to combine.

Now add the sliced onions and peppers (bell peppers) and fry for about two minutes until the onions are translucent and soft. Add the garlic and ginger paste, chillies, turmeric and mixed powder or Kashmiri paste, followed by the tomato purée. Let these sizzle for a minute and then stir in the rest of the vegatbles to fry for a couple of minutes, stirring continuously.

Pour in the base curry sauce and simmer undisturbed, stirring only if it is catching to the pan.

When the vegetables are cooked to your liking, add the tomato wedges and dried fenugreek leaves. Season with salt and pepper to taste and sprinkle with the garam masala to serve.

TIP: A couple of pre-cooked potatoes (page 29) and a little of the cooking sauce is a nice addition.

This is a typical Bangladeshi restaurant version of aloo gobi. Potatoes and cauliflower go so well together. Who'd have thought? Although I usually use rapeseed oil in my curries, I do prefer ghee with this one – the buttery flavour is delicious with the vegetables.

ALOO GOBI
SERVES 4 OR MORE AS PART OF A MULTI-COURSE MEAL

4 tbsp ghee, rapeseed oil or seasoned oil (see p7)
½ tsp brown mustard seeds
3 green cardamom pods, lightly bruised
1 tsp cumin seeds
½ tsp panch poran (see p16)
About 20 fresh or frozen curry leaves
1 onion, finely chopped
2 tbsp garlic and ginger paste (see p18)
2 fresh green chillies, finely chopped
1½ tbsp mixed powder (see p17)
½ tsp ground turmeric
1 tsp chilli powder
1 tsp amchoor (dried mango powder)
7 tbsp tomato purée (see p19)
500ml (2 cups) base curry sauce (see p22), heated
300g (10½ oz) pre-cooked potato chunks (see p29), plus 150ml (scant ⅔ cup) of their cooking stock, or more curry sauce
300g (10½ oz) cauliflower, steamed until just over half cooked
1 large tomato, roughly diced
½ tsp garam masala (see p14)
1 tsp dried fenugreek (methi) leaves
4 tbsp finely chopped coriander (cilantro)
Salt

Heat the ghee or oil in a pan over a medium-high heat and, when very hot, add the mustard seeds. When they begin to crackle, throw in the cardamom pods, cumin seeds, panch poran and curry leaves. When your kitchen becomes fragrant with the aroma of all these delicious ingredients, add the onion and fry for a couple of minutes, then stir in the garlic and ginger paste and the green chillies.

The pan will sizzle as these ingredients release their moisture. When it all quietens down, stir in the mixed powder, turmeric, chilli powder and amchoor, followed immediately by the tomato purée.

Pour in 250ml (1 cup) of the base curry sauce and let it bubble for a minute or so, without stirring. Add the pre-cooked potatoes, cauliflower and the rest of the base curry sauce with the stock. Simmer until the cauliflower is cooked through and your sauce is your desired consistency, adding more stock or base sauce if it becomes too dry.

To finish, add the diced tomato and season with salt to taste. Swirl in the garam masala and dried fenugreek leaves and top with the chopped coriander (cilantro).

This makes a nice side dish and is also very good served as a vegetarian main course. The bindi (okra) should be cooked through but still have a good crunch to them.

BINDI MASALA
SERVES 4 OR MORE AS PART OF A MULTI-COURSE MEAL

3 tbsp rapeseed oil or seasoned oil (see p7)
1½ tbsp panch poran (see p16)
3 Kashmiri dried red chillies
1 red onion, finely chopped
2–3 fresh green chillies, to taste, finely chopped
2 tbsp garlic and ginger paste (see p18)
1 tsp amchoor (dried mango powder)
1 tsp coconut flour
1 firm plum tomato, roughly chopped
450g (1 lb) fresh okra, sliced into discs
250ml (1 cup) base curry sauce (see p22), heated
Juice of 1 lemon
2 tbsp freshly grated coconut (optional)
Salt

Heat the oil in a pan over a medium-high heat until bubbly hot. Add the panch poran and dried chillies, and sizzle for about 30 seconds until fragrant. Stir in the onion and green chillies, and sauté until the onion is soft and translucent. Add the garlic and ginger paste and fry for another 30 seconds.

Sprinkle in the amchoor and coconut flour, followed by the tomato and okra. Let the okra fry for a couple of minutes until hot but still crisp then pour in the base curry sauce. Turn the heat up and let the sauce bubble until you are happy with the consistency.

To serve, season with salt to taste and squeeze the lemon juice over the top. Sprinkle with the freshly grated coconut, if you like.

I make this popular vegetarian curry two ways depending on my mood. You could blend the spinach and chillies with a little spice stock or water to make a smooth spinach purée as in the lamb saag recipe (see page 72). Alternatively, you could make it as shown with blanched, roughly cut baby spinach leaves.

I like to use coconut oil for this one, which is now widely available. It adds a nice, nutty flavour to the curry.

SAAG ALOO

SERVES 2 AS A MAIN COURSE OR 4 AS A SIDE DISH

2 tablespoons coconut oil, rapeseed or seasoned oil (see p7)
1 tsp cumin seeds
10 fresh or frozen curry leaves
1 onion, finely chopped
1–3 green chillies, to taste
A pinch of turmeric
1 tsp black onion seeds (nigella seeds)
2 tablespoons garlic and ginger paste (see p18)
20 cherry tomatoes, halved
2 large pre-cooked stewed potatoes (see p29) and 200ml (¾ cup) of their cooking stock
200g (7 oz) fresh baby leaf spinach, blanched for 30 seconds and roughly chopped
1 tsp garam masala
Salt and freshly ground pepper

Heat the oil in a large wok or frying pan over medium-high heat. When it begins to bubble, add the cumin seeds and allow to sizzle until fragrant. About 30 seconds should do.

Now add the curry leaves followed by the chopped onion, green chillies, turmeric and onion seeds and continue frying until the onion is soft and translucent. Stir in the garlic and ginger paste.

Add the cherry tomatoes and mix it all up well. Then, add the pre-cooked potatoes and their cooking stock and simmer for a few minutes until the sauce has thickened and the potatoes are heated through.

Stir in the chopped spinach. If using the puréed spinach and chilli method, this is the time to pour it in.

Simmer for another minute or so until you are happy with the consistency. If you prefer more sauce, add some more cooking stock or even a little base curry sauce (see page 22).

Sprinkle the garam masala over the top and season with salt and pepper to taste.

This is an authentic Punjabi muttar paneer recipe but with a British twist. In this version, the sauce is blended until silky smooth. We do like our smooth sauces here in the UK.

It's worth noting that this sauce is not limited to paneer and peas. It goes well with so many other main ingredients. Prawns (shrimp), chicken, bite-sized pieces of seekh kebab... If you think it sounds good, it will be.

MUTTAR PANEER

SERVES 4 OR MORE AS PART OF A MULTI-COURSE MEAL

1kg (2¼ lb) paneer (see p30 for homemade), cut into 4cm (1½ in) cubes
1 tbsp rapeseed oil
2 tbsp garlic and ginger paste (see p18)
1 tsp salt
Juice of 1 lemon
2 tsp chilli powder
5 tbsp Greek yoghurt, whisked
¼ tsp garam masala (see p14)

FOR THE SAUCE
3 tbsp rapeseed oil or seasoned oil (see p7)
4 green cardamom pods, lightly bruised
2 cloves
1 bay leaf
2 large onions, finely chopped
3 tbsp garlic and ginger paste (see p18)
1.2kg (2¾ lb) tomatoes, halved
2 tbsp raw cashew paste (see p19)
1 tbsp chilli powder, or to taste
2 fresh green chillies, quartered
150g (1 cup) frozen peas
5 tbsp single (light) cream
¼ tsp garam masala (see p14)
80g (⅓ cup) cold butter, diced
Juice of 1 lemon
2 tsp dried fenugreek (methi) leaves, crushed
Salt

Put the paneer in a bowl with the oil, garlic and ginger paste, salt, lemon juice and chilli powder, and mix gently to coat. Set aside for about 15 minutes then stir in the whisked yoghurt and garam masala. Leave to marinate while you prepare the tomato sauce.

In a large saucepan, heat the oil until hot. Toss in the cardamom pods, cloves and bay leaf, and sizzle for 30 seconds. Add the onions and fry for a further 3 minutes until soft and translucent but not browned. Stir in the garlic and ginger paste.

Fry for another 30 seconds, stirring, then add the tomatoes, 125ml (½ cup) water and the cashew paste. Let this come to a simmer and cook until the onions and tomatoes break down into a thick sauce, about 5 minutes. Using a jug or hand-held blender, blend until super smooth, about 3–4 minutes.

Return the sauce to the pan and stir in the chilli powder and green chillies. Let this all come to a mild bubble then add the paneer cubes and peas, and heat through for about 2 minutes (if you cook the cheese too long, it will begin to disintegrate into the sauce, so watch carefully).

To finish, swirl in the cream and garam masala, then stir in the cold butter one piece at a time. Stir in the lemon juice and check for seasoning, adding salt to taste. Top with the dried fenugreek leaves and serve.

TIP: My pan-fried paneer (see page 30) and grilled paneer (page 105) can be substituted for the raw marinated paneer with equally tasty results.

Monday nights are always curry nights at my house. On Sundays, we usually cook up a roast Sunday dinner with all the fixings, so I always make extra roast potatoes for this curry. You could do the same in place of the pre-cooked stewed potatoes used here, although the cooking stock is nice added to this sauce.

Bombay aloo can be served either quite saucy or dry, and as I usually serve this curry as a side dish, my sauce is on the dry side. If serving as a vegetarian main course, you might want to add more liquid.

BOMBAY ALOO
SERVES 4 OR MORE AS PART OF A MULTI-COURSE MEAL

4 tbsp ghee, rapeseed oil or seasoned oil (see p7)
1 tsp cumin seeds
1 onion, finely chopped
2 tbsp garlic and ginger paste (see p18)
7 tbsp tomato purée (see p19)
300ml (1¼ cups) base curry sauce, heated (or more for a saucier dish, see introduction)
600g (1¼ lb) pre-cooked stewed potatoes (see p29), cut into bite-sized chunks, plus 100ml (⅓ cup) of the cooking stock, or water
1 tbsp mixed powder (see p17)
1 tsp chilli powder
2 tomatoes, quartered
1 tsp dried fenugreek (methi) leaves
½ tsp garam masala (see p14)
3 tbsp finely chopped coriander (cilantro)
Salt

Heat the ghee or oil in a pan over a medium-high heat then add the cumin seeds. When they become fragrant, stir in the onion and fry for about 3 minutes until soft and translucent. Stir in the garlic and ginger paste and enjoy that garlicky aroma.

Now stir in the tomato purée, base curry sauce and potato cooking stock or water, and bring to a simmer. There is no need to stir unless it is obviously catching on the pan. Scrape any caramelized sauce on the sides of the pan back in then add the pre-cooked potatoes, mixed powder and chilli powder.

Continue to simmer while spooning the sauce over the potatoes. When well coated, add the tomatoes and cook for a further couple of minutes.

Season with salt to taste and sprinkle with the dried fenugreek leaves and garam masala. Top with the chopped coriander (cilantro) to serve.

This has to be one of the most ordered side dishes at Indian restaurants. Personally, I feel the meal just isn't complete without a good tarka dhal. A 'tarka' is a mixture of spices and/or aromatics that are tempered in oil or ghee. This mixture is then poured over the cooked dhal just before serving. So the channa dhal (see page 119) is actually a tarka dhal too.

For this quick and easy version, I use masoor dhal (split small red lentils), which, unlike other lentils, need only to be washed and rinsed under cold water before cooking. You can also use the finished tarka dhal in my chicken dhansak recipe (see page 67) instead of plain dhal.

TARKA DHAL
SERVES 4 OR MORE AS PART OF A MULTI-COURSE MEAL

250g (1½ cups) masoor dhal, rinsed
3 tbsp ghee
10 fresh or frozen curry leaves
1 tsp cumin seeds
1 cinnamon stick
1 onion, finely sliced
4 garlic cloves, finely chopped
2 tbsp garam masala (see p14)
½ tsp ground turmeric
Salt and freshly ground pepper

Put the dhal into a pan and pour over about 400ml (1⅔ cups) water. Simmer over a medium-high heat for about 25 minutes until tender, removing any foam that forms on the top.

Meanwhile, melt the ghee in a frying pan and add the curry leaves, cumin seeds and cinnamon stick. Stir this all up so that the ghee soaks up the flavour of the spices. Add the onion and fry for about 5 minutes until light brown. Add the garlic, garam masala and turmeric, and sizzle until the garlic is soft.

Season the cooked dhal with salt and pepper, then pour the ghee mixture (the tarka) over the lentils to serve.

This recipe was inspired by a visit to Prashad in Bradford. The head chef Minal Patel showed me her recipe for channa dhal and it was amazing. She used four different types of lentils, cooked separately then blended together with all the other ingredients.

Usually, the channa dhal you get at a curry house is made simply from channa lentils, so I've simplified Minal's recipe a little for you here. If you like channa dhal, you're going to love this one.

CHANNA DHAL

SERVES 4 OR MORE AS PART OF A MULTI-COURSE MEAL

300g (1⅔ cups) channa dhal, soaked in water for 30 minutes
About 1 tbsp rapeseed oil or seasoned oil (see p7)
3 tbsp ghee
½ tsp brown mustard seeds
1 tsp cumin seeds
Pinch of asafoetida
1 tsp ground turmeric
½ onion, finely chopped
5 garlic cloves, cut into slivers
1 tbsp garlic and ginger paste (see p18)
1–5 fresh green bullet chillies, to taste, finely chopped
3 tomatoes, roughly chopped
1 tbsp ground coriander
½ tsp ground cumin
½ tsp garam masala (see p14)
Salt
Chopped fresh coriander (cilantro), to serve

Drain the lentils and rinse in several changes of water, then place in a saucepan with 700ml (3 cups) fresh water. Bring to a boil and drizzle the oil on top to stop the water from foaming over the top.

Reduce the heat and simmer until the lentils are soft but with just a little bite to them, 45–60 minutes, skimming off any foam that does form. Do not strain; allow the water to reduce down.

Meanwhile, in a separate pan, melt the ghee over a high heat. When it is visibly very hot, toss in the mustard seeds. They will begin to pop. Reduce the heat to medium-high and add the cumin seeds and asafoetida. Temper in the oil for about 30 seconds and then add the turmeric and onion and fry until soft and translucent, 3–5 minutes should do the job. Stir in the slivered garlic, garlic and ginger paste and chillies, and cook, stirring continuously, for another 30 seconds.

Returning to the dhal, reduce the heat to medium and stir in the chopped tomatoes, coriander and cumin, and bring to a happy simmer. Keep warm.

You can leave the dhal as it is once cooked, or whisk or blend until creamy. Stir the onion and ghee mixture into the lentils and sprinkle with garam masala. To serve, add salt to taste and top with a little chopped coriander (cilantro).

CHEF'S SPECIALS

On the following pages, you will find some of the dishes that have made a big impression on me. Some are authentic recipes from the subcontinent and others are simply fun creations that needed to be shared.

This is an interesting curry. There is no garlic, ginger or onion in the mix, which is unusual here in the UK. The flavour comes from the warming spices that are sizzled in hot ghee. That and a simple but delicious marinade. Boti murgh malai is Bangladeshi in origin and a lot different to what you find on the menus at most Indian restaurants.

This recipe calls for Kashmiri paste. There are some really good commercial brands available, but you could also make your own if you really want to impress. See my recipe on page 15.

BOTI MURGH MALAI
SERVES 4 OR MORE AS PART OF A MULTI-COURSE MEAL

4 skinless, boneless
  chicken breasts, diced
  into bite-sized pieces
2 tbsp ghee
2 Indian bay leaves
  (cassia leaves)
2 green cardamom pods,
  lightly bruised
2 cloves
1 star anise
1 cinnamon stick
1–2 tbsp Kashmiri paste
  (good-quality shop-bought,
  or see p15 for homemade)
  to taste
250ml (1 cup) single
  (light) cream
4 tomatoes, quartered
3 tbsp finely chopped
  coriander (cilantro),
  plus extra to serve
Salt and freshly ground pepper

FOR THE MARINADE
Juice of ½ lemon
100g (½ cup) plain yoghurt
1 tsp salt
½ tsp ground turmeric
1 tsp paprika
1 tsp ground cumin
1 tsp chilli powder
1 tsp ground coriander
2 tbsp mixed powder (see p17)

To make the marinade, put the lemon juice, yoghurt, salt, turmeric, paprika, cumin, chilli powder, coriander and mixed powder into a large bowl and whisk until nice and smooth. Mix in the chicken, cover and marinate in the fridge for at least 3 hours and up to 24 hours; the longer the better.

When ready to cook, remove the chicken from the marinade, reserving the marinade, place on a rack under a hot grill (broiler) and cook until the exterior of the chicken is slightly blackened and the meat is almost cooked through. Set aside while you make the sauce.

Heat the ghee in a large frying pan and, when hot, add the bay leaves, cardamom pods, cloves, star anise and cinnamon stick, and fry for about a minute. Plop in the Kashmiri paste and stir to combine. Fry for a further couple of minutes.

Pour in the cream and the reserved marinade, then stir in the chicken. Add about 100ml (⅓ cup) water and coat the meat with the sauce. Add the tomato quarters and coriander (cilantro).

Cook for a further 5–10 minutes. The sauce will thicken and you will be left with a delicious curry like no other! Season with salt and pepper to taste and sprinkle with coriander.

The simple stir-fried biryanis served at most curry houses simply don't compare to this slow-cooked kacchi biryani. I first tried it back in 2013 at Sheba on Brick Lane in London. It was so good I had to get the recipe! This is my take on their delicious and hugely popular dish.

KACCHI LAMB BIRYANI

SERVES 6–8

3 onions, finely sliced and fried (see p19), cooking oil reserved
1 leg of lamb, cut through the bone into 12 or more pieces*

FOR THE MARINADE
2 tbsp garlic and ginger paste (see p18)
420g (2 cups) plain yoghurt
Juice of 2 lemons
2 fresh green chillies, roughly chopped
1 tbsp ground cumin
1 tbsp garam masala (see p14)
½ tsp ground turmeric
1 tsp ground cinnamon
¼ tsp ground mace
½ tsp chilli powder
30g (1 oz) fresh coriander (cilantro) leaves, chopped
10g (⅓ oz) fresh mint leaves, chopped

FOR THE RICE
2 tbsp sea salt
Whole garam masala (1 cinnamon stick, 10 peppercorns, 1 bay leaf, 1 tbsp cumin seeds)
500g (1 lb) aged basmati rice
Pinch of saffron threads infused with 300ml (1¼ cups) hot milk
60g (2 oz) fresh coriander (cilantro) leaves, chopped
20g (⅔ oz) fresh mint leaves, chopped
6 tbsp melted ghee
1 tbsp rose water
½ tsp ground cumin
Dried rose petals (optional)

Mix the marinade ingredients in a bowl with a quarter of the fried onions and 200ml (¾ cup) of cooled reserved oil. Add the lamb and rub the marinade into it. Cover and marinate overnight in the fridge.

To make the rice, when ready to cook, bring 1.5 litres (6 cups) water to a boil in a large pan. Add the salt, whole garam masala and rice, and simmer for 6 minutes. After the 6 minutes, remove half the rice from the water with a strainer and place in a small bowl. Cook the remaining rice for another minute and remove to a second bowl.

Now spoon about 3 tbsp of the reserved onion oil into a large, heavy-based saucepan and tip in the marinated meat and all of the marinade. Spread the first batch of rice, including any whole spices over the lamb. Cover with half the remaining fried onions and half the chopped coriander (cilantro) and mint.

Add the second bowl of rice on top and then the remaining fried onions and herbs. Spoon the melted ghee over the top layer, followed by the saffron-infused milk, the rose water and a sprinkle of cumin powder. Scatter some dried rose petals on top, if using.

Make a soft dough with water and flour and run it around the top of the pan and secure the lid tightly on top. Heat the biryani over a high heat for a couple of minutes. When you hear it simmering, reduce the heat to very low and cook for about 40 minutes. Don't be tempted to lift the lid.

After 40 minutes, your kitchen will smell amazing. Take your biryani to the table and unseal the lid. Lift it and enjoy the amazing aroma. Stir the meat from the bottom into the rice about three or four times and serve with your favourite raita.

* **TIP:** Ask your butcher to cut your leg of lamb into pieces.

This recipe was sent to me by my friend Usman Butt – executive chef of Imran's in Birmingham's Balti Triangle. If you're a lamb curry fan, this is one you've simply got to try. The sauce is quite mild and has a delicious flavour that when teamed with the tender lamb shanks is about as good as it gets.

Lamb nihari is a fantastic all-round option for entertaining. Your guests can add chopped green chillies, lemon juice, julienned ginger and fresh coriander (cilantro) to taste at the table. If you want the curry to be fiery hot, add loads of chillies, or simply go for some of the less spicy options to produce the perfect curry for you.

LAMB NIHARI
SERVES 4

4 lamb shanks, about 2kg (4½ lb) in total
125ml (½ cup) rapeseed oil or seasoned oil (see p7)
1 whole nutmeg, crushed into smaller pieces
1 tbsp mace blades
2 tbsp fennel seeds
3 Indian bay leaves (cassia leaves), shredded
2.5cm (1 in) piece of cinnamon stick or cassia bark, broken into small pieces
1 tsp black peppercorns
1 tsp nigella seeds (black onion seeds)
1 tsp cloves
2 tsp cumin seeds
1 tsp paprika
1 tsp hot chilli powder
1 tsp ground ginger
40g (1½ oz) unsalted butter
1 onion, sliced into rings
2 generous tsp chapatti flour
Salt

GARNISHES FOR THE TABLE
4 tbsp (or more) fine julienne of ginger
2–3 hot fresh green chillies, finely sliced
Handful of coriander (cilantro) leaves
Lemon wedges

Place the lamb shanks on a plate and rub them all over with ½ tsp salt and 1 tsp of the oil. Set aside while you prepare the spice masala.

This is a raw spice masala so no need to roast the spices first. Put the nutmeg, mace, fennel seeds, bay leaves, cinnamon, peppercorns, nigella seeds, cloves and cumin seeds in a spice grinder and grind to a fine powder. Stir in the paprika, chilli powder and ground ginger.

Melt the butter in a large saucepan with a tight-fitting lid over a medium heat. Add the onion rings and fry for about 5 minutes until soft, translucent and lightly browned. Transfer to a plate with a slotted spoon and set aside.

Now pour the remaining oil into the saucepan and brown the lamb shanks for about 2 minutes.

Add the browned onions coated with the spices and pour in 1.2 litres (4¾ cups) warm water.

Arrange the lamb shanks in the saucepan, cover and simmer over a low heat for 3 hours, basting and turning the shanks every 30 minutes. After 3 hours, carefully lift out the shanks into a large, warmed serving bowl. Skim off as much excess oil from the cooking liquid as possible from the sauce and discard.

Mix the chapatti flour with 4 teaspoons water to make a smooth paste. Whisk the paste into the sauce and simmer for 5–6 minutes to thicken. Check for seasoning, add salt to taste and then pour the sauce over the meat in the serving bowl. Serve the garnishes in little bowls on the table to add to the lamb nihari as you like.

Whenever I go out to a Bangladeshi-run curry house, I look for their shatkora curries. I absolutely love the intensely tangy shatkora fruit. These are available frozen from Asian grocers and, when in season, they can often be purchased fresh. If you have trouble finding them, you could substitute shatkora pickle or, if all else fails, quartered limes, but the flavour will not be the same.

This is a popular beef curry that, when prepared like this, is usually made in bulk and promoted as a house special. Not only does the beef need to cook until tender, but the shatkora require a long simmer so that they are not tough, and also to release their flavour into the sauce. Only the rind of the fruit is used, because the pulp is terribly bitter. If you have a couple beef marrow bones, throw them into the dish as it simmers.

This recipe was inspired by a visit to Omar's, a small curry house in Hatfield Peverel. It may be small but the curries I enjoyed there are right up there with the best!

SYLHETI BEEF
SERVES 4 OR MORE AS PART OF A MULTI-COURSE MEAL

3 tbsp rapeseed oil or seasoned oil (see p7)
2 black cardamom pods, lightly bruised
1 large onion, finely chopped
2 tbsp garlic and ginger paste (see p18)
3 tbsp tomato purée (see p19)
1 tsp each of ground turmeric, cumin and coriander (cilantro), medium chilli powder and paprika
800g (1¾ lb) beef topside, cut into bite-sized pieces, (see Note)
750ml (3 cups) spice stock (see p18), plus a little more if required
¼ shatkora, outer rind only, cut into small pieces
1 tsp garam masala (see p14)
Chopped coriander (cilantro) leaves, to finish
Salt

Heat the oil in a large frying pan over a medium-high heat. When hot, toss in the cardamom pods and, after about 30 seconds, add the onion and fry for 5 minutes until soft, translucent and lightly browned.

Now add the garlic and ginger paste and fry for a further minute, stirring. Add the tomato purée and the ground spices, and cook for another minute. Add the beef and about 250ml (1 cup) of the spice stock. Boil it all for about 5 minutes then add the remaining spice stock and the shatkora rind.

Reduce the heat and simmer for 45–60 minutes, or until the sauce reduces to a fairly thick consistency and the meat is tender. Add more spice stock if needed.

To serve, add the garam masala, and salt to taste and top with the chopped coriander (cilantro).

NOTE: In the UK, most people prefer their curries cooked with meat off the bone, but this recipe is sometimes made using beef ribs. If you like ribs, give them a go. You'll love the beefy ribs in this sauce.

I like this curry not just for its fantastic flavour but also the different textures. I love biting into the tender meatballs and chickpeas, covered in the mildly spiced sauce. Prepare the meat for the koftas as in the seekh kebab recipe on page 96. I love the way these are steamed on top of the onions, giving them a completely different texture to the grilled seekh kebabs.

LAMB KOFTA AND CHICKPEA CURRY
SERVES 4 OR MORE AS PART OF A MULTI-COURSE MEAL

FOR THE KOFTA

700g (1½ lb) lamb mince
1 egg
2 tbsp green chilli paste
   (see p18)
2 onions, finely chopped
1 tbsp freshly roasted ground
   coriander (see p12)
1 tbsp garam masala (see p14)
Large bunch of coriander
   (cilantro), finely chopped
1 tsp salt

FOR THE CURRY

4 tbsp rapeseed oil or
   seasoned oil (see p7)
3 onions, finely chopped
2 tbsp garlic and ginger paste
   (see p18)
4 large tomatoes, finely chopped
1 tbsp ground coriander
1 tsp chilli powder
1 tsp ground turmeric
2 fresh green chillies,
   halved lengthways
1 tbsp garam masala (see p14)
1 x 400g tin (1½ cups)
   chickpeas, drained
Small bunch of coriander
   (cilantro), chopped
1 tsp chopped mint (optional)
Salt

Following the method on page 96, knead the lamb mince and other kofta ingredients together to create a 'lace' texture. Form the mixture into koftas the size of golf balls, using your hands (dipping your fingers in a little oil or water helps to shape them).

Heat the oil in a pan over a medium heat. When nice and hot but not smoking, add the onions and fry for about 5 minutes until soft and translucent. Sprinkle with a little salt then add the koftas. Reduce the temperature to low and cover the pan.

After about 5 minutes, the koftas should be almost cooked through. Check them, moving them around carefully if required. Continue cooking, covered, for a couple more minutes, then stir in the garlic and ginger paste. Next add the tomatoes, ground coriander, chilli powder and turmeric, then the fresh chillies and stir everything to combine. If you like more sauce, you could add a little water or spice stock (see p18) at this stage.

Cover and simmer for about 5 more minutes. Check for seasoning and add the garam masala, and salt to taste. To serve, stir in the chickpeas and top with chopped coriander, and mint if you like.

Sometimes simplicity is best, and that is certainly the case with the famous lamb chops served at Lahore Kebab House in Shoreditch.

I first visited Lahore Kebab House with my friend Raj Singh, who runs a company called Secret Food Tours. One of his tours is a walk through Shoreditch and Brick Lane where he takes people to three of the best restaurants in the area as well as a few other interesting stops. He offered to take me on his tour one evening and our last stop was Lahore Kebab House.

Lahore Kebab house is a massive restaurant on two levels, with seating for 350. On Friday and Saturday nights, those seats are all filled many times over. After trying their amazing chilli paneer, grilled lamb chops and chicken tikka, I made arrangements to return and meet one of the owners, Emran Siddique.

The restaurant is a family-run business that has been serving high-quality Pakistani food for over 40 years. Sure, they do feature a few of the British classic curries on their menu, but they are most famous for their traditional Pakistani dishes.

When there, you can watch the chefs prepare huge karahis of mouthwatering curry. These delicious marinated lamb chops are cooked over a flame grill, which produces a tasty char. They are out-of-this-world gorgeous!

GRILLED LAMB CHOPS
SERVES 4 OR MORE AS PART OF A MULTI-COURSE MEAL

1 tbsp rapeseed oil
1 tbsp green chilli paste
    (see p18)
2 tbsp garlic and ginger paste
    (see p18)
1 tbsp garam masala
    (see p14)
½ tsp ground turmeric
1 tsp chilli powder
Juice of 1 lemon
8–10 lamb chops on the bone,
    with most surface fat removed
100g (½ cup) Greek yoghurt
Fresh coriander (cilantro),
    to serve
Salt and black freshly
    ground pepper

In a large glass or ceramic bowl, mix the oil, chilli paste, garlic and ginger paste, garam masala, turmeric, chilli powder and lemon juice together. Add the lamb chops and massage the marinade into the meat. Let this stand for about 20 minutes.

Whisk the yoghurt until nice and creamy then pour it over the meat, ensuring every piece is coated. Marinate the meat for 24–72 hours. (You could marinate for a shorter time but the longer the better.)

When ready to cook, set up your barbecue for direct heat cooking (see page 88), until the coals are extremely hot. Grill each lamb chop until nicely charred underneath then flip over and do the same on the other side. When nicely blackened, remove from the heat to rest for about 5 minutes. Season with salt and pepper and serve garnished with fresh coriander (cilantro).

NOTE: The char-grilled exterior of these lamb chops is one of the things that makes them so delicious. I don't recommend pan-frying.

Xacutti is one of the most popular Indian dishes from Goa. As with many of the authentic dishes from the Indian subcontinent, restaurateurs here in the UK have taken to reinventing it with spices and techniques that they prefer to use. Sho-coo-tee is the Bangladeshi pronunciation of xacutti and this version is just as good as, if not better, than the original.

The use of curry leaves and coconut milk are very Goan, but the panch poran and minced lamb rolled into the chicken breast give it a unique and delightful Bangladeshi touch. The chicken roulades are not terribly difficult to make, but if you want to make it even easier on yourself, simple chicken tikka is a delicious alternative.

SHO-COO-TEE
SERVES 4 OR MORE AS PART OF A MULTI-COURSE MEAL

15–20 cherry tomatoes, halved
3 tbsp rapeseed oil or seasoned oil (see p7)
3 tbsp ghee
1 tbsp panch poran (see p16)
3 Indian bay leaves (cassia leaves)
10 fresh curry leaves
2 tbsp garlic and ginger paste (see p18)
3 fresh green bullet chillies, finely chopped
1 tsp paprika
Pinch of ground turmeric
1 quantity fried onions (see p19)
400ml (1¾ cups) thick coconut milk
1–2 tbsp date molasses or regular molasses, to taste
8 skinless, boneless, large chicken breasts, sliced horizontally into 2 equal-sized, flat pieces
400g (14 oz) raw minced lamb prepared as with seekh kebabs (see p96)
1 tbsp garam masala (see p14)
4 tbsp chopped coriander (cilantro)
Salt and freshly ground pepper

Preheat the oven to 140°C/275°F/gas mark 1. Put the tomatoes cut side up in a baking tray, sprinkle with 1 tbsp of the oil and some salt and pepper. Bake for about 60 minutes or until reduced in size by about a third. Set aside.

Melt the ghee in a large saucepan over a medium-high heat. Toss in the panch poran, bay and curry leaves and let it all sizzle for about 30 seconds. Add the garlic and ginger paste, fresh chillies, paprika and turmeric and fry for a further 30 seconds.

Add the baked tomatoes, fried onions, coconut milk and molasses (date molasses is intensely sweet). Simmer for 5 minutes over a low heat, stirring continuously. Blend this sauce until silky smooth. Set aside or refrigerate until ready to cook the chicken.

Using a meat mallet, pound each chicken breast half until thin and flat. Place one of the flattened breast halves in the centre of a large piece of cling film (plastic wrap). Spread about 3 tbsp of the prepared minced lamb down the centre and wrap the chicken breast around the lamb, into a sausage shape. Twist the ends of the cling film to ensure the meat is tightly wrapped. Repeat with the other chicken breast halves.

Bring a large pan of water to a boil and place the roulades in it. Simmer for about 10 minutes until completely cooked through. Using a slotted spoon, transfer the roulades to a plate. Unwrap and slice the roulades into bite-sized pieces. Heat the remaining oil in a frying pan and sear the roulade pieces on the cut ends.

Bring the blended sauce to a simmer and stir in the roulade pieces. Check for seasoning and stir in the garam masala. Serve topped with the chopped coriander (cilantro).

In 1947, Kundan Lal Gujral opened the first tandoori restaurant, called Moti Mahal, in Delhi, India. Although tandoor-style ovens had already been used for thousands of years, he was the first to have large tandoors manufactured for use in a restaurant. The restaurant served delicious marinated chicken, meat and vegetables, all charred to perfection in a tandoor. Not one to waste, Gujral came up with the idea of using the leftover marinades in a curry, and butter chicken (murgh makhani) was born. For the chicken, use Tandoori Chicken Tikka (see page 92) or Tandoori Chicken Legs (see page 46). Reserve the marinade for the sauce.

BUTTER CHICKEN
SERVES 4 OR MORE AS PART OF A MULTI-COURSE MEAL

1.5kg (3 lb 5 oz) grilled tandoori chicken (see p92 or 93)

FOR THE BUTTER CHICKEN SAUCE
4 tbsp rapeseed oil or seasoned oil (see page 7)
2.5cm (1in) piece of cinnamon stick or cassia bark
2 star anise
6 green cardamom pods, lightly bruised
2 Indian bay leaves (cassia leaves)
2 onions, finely chopped
1 carrot, grated
2 tbsp garlic and ginger paste (see p18)
2 x 400g tins (4 cups) chopped tomatoes
1 tsp paprika
1 tbsp ground cumin
1 tbsp ground coriander
1 tsp ground turmeric
300ml (1¼ cups) double (heavy) cream
3 tbsp butter, chilled
1 tbsp garam masala (see p14)
Salt and freshly ground pepper

Heat the oil in a large saucepan over medium-high heat. When hot, toss in the cinnamon stick, star anise, cardamom pods and bay leaves, and stir them in the oil for about 30 seconds.

Now add the onions and carrot, and fry for about 15 minutes, stirring occasionally, so that the onions turn soft and translucent but not browned. Sprinkle 1 tsp salt over the top to help release some of the moisture from the onions. Now add the garlic and ginger paste and fry for 30 seconds, followed by the chopped tomatoes.

Add the paprika and the ground cumin, coriander and turmeric, and simmer for about 3 minutes. At this stage you have a choice. You can either leave the sauce as it is or take the whole spices out and blend it to a smooth sauce. I'll leave that one to you. I usually leave it as is.

Lower the heat to medium and place the grilled chicken pieces in the sauce to heat through. To finish, whisk in the cream and reserved marinade from preparing the chicken, and turn the heat back up to medium-high. Add the chilled butter, 1 tbsp at a time, and check for seasoning, adding more salt if needed. Sprinkle with the garam masala and serve.

Kolkata-style prawn curries are making their way onto many curry-house menus. This recipe was inspired by a visit to my local curry house, Raj Bari in Yarm. I didn't see the chefs making the dish while I was there, but they were nice enough to let me know what went into it. I returned home and decided to make the curry all over again for my family. It was that good!

KOLKATA (CALCUTTA) PRAWNS
SERVES 4 OR MORE AS PART OF A MULTI-COURSE MEAL

500g (1 lb) raw tiger prawns (shrimp), peeled and deveined
½ tsp ground turmeric
2 tbsp ghee or mustard oil
1 tsp black mustard seeds
3 green cardamom pods, lightly bruised
4 cloves
1 cinnamon stick
1 bay leaf
20 fresh curry leaves
2 shallots, finely chopped
2 tbsp garlic and ginger paste (see p18)
1 fresh green chilli, halved lengthways and deseeded
2 tbsp coconut flour
400ml (1¾ cups) coconut milk
Pinch of saffron threads
½ tsp paprika
1 tsp garam masala (see p14)
1 tbsp finely chopped coriander (cilantro)
Salt

Sprinkle the prawns (shrimp) with the turmeric and mix well. Heat the ghee or oil in a large frying pan or wok over a medium-high heat. When hot, toss in the mustard seeds. When they begin to pop, reduce the heat to medium and add the rest of the whole spices, bay leaf and curry leaves. Fry for 30 seconds then add the shallots and sauté for about 5 minutes, until translucent and soft.

Add the garlic and ginger paste and the fresh chilli, and stir to combine. Add the prawns and paprika and fry, stirring regularly until the prawns begin to turn pink. Stir in the coconut flour, coconut milk and saffron and simmer for a further few minutes so that the sauce thickens slightly and the prawns cook through. To serve, stir in the garam masala, check for seasoning and add salt to taste. Top with the fresh coriander (cilantro).

This is a flavour combo not to be missed. The spicy pineapple chutney teamed with the prawn curry just plain gets it. I like to serve Ana Chingri in the hallowed-out pineapples just as Chef Eshan 'Mo' Miah suggested I do. I'm not one to pass up good advice and I've been serving this curry in pineapples ever since. Feel free to use bowls though.

ANA CHINGRI (PRAWN WITH PINEAPPLE)

SERVES 2 OR MORE AS PART OF A MULTI-COURSE MEAL

6 garlic cloves, unpeeled
1 pineapple
½ tsp roasted cumin seeds (see p12)
4 fresh green chillies, very finely chopped
4 tbsp chopped coriander (cilantro), plus extra to serve
2 tbsp rapeseed oil
1 tsp mustard seeds
½ onion, finely chopped
1 tbsp garlic paste (see p18)
2 Indian bay leaves (cassia leaves)
1 tsp ground cumin
1 tsp chilli powder
½ tsp ground turmeric
1 tomato, chopped
2 tbsp tomato purée (see p19)
500g (1 lb) raw prawns (shrimp), shelled and deveined
Juice of 1 lime
Salt

Roast the garlic cloves directly over a gas hob flame on a skewer or in a dry frying pan, turning them as they roast, until blackened all over. Set aside to cool.

Using a large, sharp knife, cut the pineapple in half lengthways and scoop out most of the flesh from the centre. Place the scooped-out pineapple in a blender, add the cumin seeds and ½ tsp salt, and squeeze the roasted garlic out of their skins into the blender. Blend to a paste then transfer to a bowl.

Add the fresh chillies and chopped coriander (cilantro) to the pineapple paste and mix well. Reserve 2 tbsp for the curry and store the rest in the fridge until ready to serve.

Heat the oil in a large saucepan over a high heat and add the mustard seeds. They will begin to pop. When they do, reduce the heat to medium-high and add the onion along with a pinch of salt. Fry until translucent and soft, then stir in the garlic paste and fry for a further 30 seconds.

Add 4 tbsp water, the bay leaves, cumin, chilli powder, turmeric and the reserved 2 tbsp pineapple paste. Cook for a further 2 minutes then add the chopped tomato and tomato purée.

Throw in the prawns (shrimp) and stir into the sauce until cooked through. Check for seasoning and spoon into the hollowed-out pineapples. Top with chopped coriander and a squeeze of lime juice, and serve with the spicy pineapple paste, and some homemade naans or chapatis (see pages 146–150).

ACCOMPANIMENTS

LIME PICKLE

MAKES APPROX. 3 × 250ML (1 CUP) JARS

There are a lot of outstanding lime pickles that can be purchased, both from small producers and big name brands. This is my recipe that I have developed over the past few years. I wouldn't say it is any better than many you can purchase but it is different and delicious. Sometimes different is good! You know you are at an outstanding restaurant if they place their own homemade pickles and chutneys on the table.

1kg (2¼ lb) limes
5 level tbsp salt
40 garlic cloves, peeled and smashed
50g ginger, very finely chopped
2 tbsp Kashmiri chilli powder

FOR THE TEMPERING
150ml (scant ⅔ cup) rapeseed oil
3 tbsp black mustard seeds
2 tbsp cumin seeds
½ tsp asafoetida

Using a fork, stab about 20 holes in each lime, then cut each lime into 8 wedges. Place in a glass bowl and add the salt, garlic, ginger and chilli powder. Mix well, coating the limes and pressing down on them to release a lot of juice. Transfer the limes to a steamer, leaving the juice in the bowl, and steam for about 15 minutes until quite soft. Transfer the steamed limes back to the glass bowl and mix back into the juices. Cover tightly with cling film (plastic wrap) and leave for 2 days in a warm place, such as a window or in direct sun outside, mixing it every 8 hours to keep the limes coated with all the other ingredients. After 2 days, heat the oil for the tempering in a large frying pan over a high heat. When very hot and almost smoking, add the mustard seeds. They will begin to pop immediately. When they do, add the cumin seeds and asafoetida, and sizzle for about 10 seconds, being careful not to burn the spices. Pour this tempered oil over the limes and mix well. Cover the bowl again with cling film and allow to sit for another 2 days in the sun, stirring

every 8 hours or so. After these last 2 days, scoop the lime pickle into a food processor and process to a chunky or smooth paste, whichever you prefer. Spoon it into sterilized jars (see below), leaving about a 5cm (2in) space at the top. The pickle should be covered with oil, so add a little extra if needed. Place the jars in a cool, dark place for 2 weeks before using. The preserved limes should keep indefinitely but, once opened, store in the fridge and use within 2 months.

HOW TO STERILIZE JARS: Preheat the oven to 110°C/225°F/gas mark ¼. If your jars have rubber sealing rings on the lid, remove them and boil in water for 5 minutes. Wash the jars thoroughly in hot, soapy water and rinse well, then place on a baking tray in the preheated oven for about 15 minutes, until dry.

KACHUMBER SALAD

MAKES: THIS MAKES ENOUGH FOR 4–6 PEOPLE AS AN ACCOMPANIMENT. YOU CAN EASILY DOUBLE OR TRIPLE THE RECIPE

This is a popular salad in many Indian restaurants. Sometimes it's on the menu but often it's simply used to garnish dishes. It makes a nice side dish as it doesn't compete with the other dishes served. It is colourful and crisp, and really helps to bring a meal together.

1 red onion, very finely diced
1 cucumber, very finely diced
1–2 tomatoes, very finely diced
1 tsp olive or vegetable oil
Juice of 1 lemon
3 tbsp finely chopped fresh coriander (cilantro)
½ tsp roasted cumin seeds (see p12)
Salt and freshly ground pepper

Mix the onion, cucumber and tomatoes together in a large bowl. Add the oil, lemon juice, chopped coriander (cilantro), cumin seeds and some salt and pepper to taste. Place in the fridge for about 30 minutes before serving.

KASHMIRI RED CHILLI AND GARLIC CHUTNEY

**MAKES ENOUGH FOR 4–6
AS AN ACCOMPANIMENT**

This is a hot one! You only need to dab a bit on your papadam and you'll see what I mean. As you can see from the ingredients list, there isn't much to this chutney. It's all about the chilli. Give it a go if you like it hot. Don't if you don't. See photograph on page 143.

20 Kashmiri dried red chillies
10 garlic cloves, peeled and smashed
½ tsp ground cumin
½ tsp salt or to taste

Split the chillies open and remove as many seeds as you can. (There's no need to remove them all as they will sink when you soak the chillies.) Toast the chillies for about a minute in a dry frying pan, pressing them down so that they are equally toasted. Tip into a bowl and add hot water from the kettle to cover. Leave to soak for 30 minutes.

Strain the chillies, reserving the soaking water, and place in a spice grinder or food processor with the garlic, cumin and salt. Taste the soaking water, and unless it is really bitter, add just enough to blend the mixture to a smooth, ketchup consistency. If the soaking water tastes bitter, discard it and use fresh water instead. Check for seasoning and it's ready to serve.

COLD ONION CHUTNEY

THIS MAKES ENOUGH FOR 4–6 PEOPLE AS AN ACCOMPANIMENT. YOU CAN EASILY DOUBLE OR TRIPLE THE RECIPE

You know those sliced onions that are served in a red sauce with papadams before the meal at Indian restaurants? Well, this simple chutney is a lot more popular than you might think, and is one of the most requested recipes on my blog. It's so easy to make.

If you're planning a curry night anytime soon, you won't want to leave this onion chutney off the menu.

1 large onion, finely sliced
3 tbsp tomato ketchup
1 tbsp tomato purée (see p19)
1 tsp chilli powder, or to taste
Pinch of salt
1 tsp roasted cumin seeds (see p12)

Put the sliced onions in a bowl of cold water with ice cubes added, and put in the fridge for about an hour. Once good and cold, drain and pat the slices dry with a clean cloth.

Now mix the ketchup, tomato purée, chilli powder and salt together. Stir in the sliced onions and roasted cumin seeds.

Stick in the fridge for about 45 minutes before serving, to allow the ingredients to get to know each other, and serve with papadams or whatever you fancy.

RED ONION CHUTNEY

THIS MAKES ENOUGH FOR 4–6 PEOPLE AS AN ACCOMPANIMENT. YOU CAN EASILY DOUBLE OR TRIPLE THE RECIPE

This onion chutney is about as easy as it gets. It's too simple for words, but then who said that delicious Indian dinners had to be complicated? Find yourself a nice, fresh red onion and it will do all the work for you. This is a very popular accompaniment, often served with papadams or piled high on kebabs and naans. It is essential to serve it very cold. See photograph on page 143.

1 large red onion, halved and finely sliced
Pinch of salt
Pinch of sugar (optional)
Juice of 1 lemon
1 fresh green chilli, finely chopped (optional)

Put the sliced onion in a bowl of cold water with ice cubes added, and put in the fridge for about an hour. Once good and cold, drain and pat the slices dry with a clean cloth.

Season with salt, and sugar if using, and squeeze the lemon juice over the top. For a spicier chutney, mix in the finely chopped chilli. Serve very cold right from the fridge.

MINT, CORIANDER AND MANGO CHUTNEY

MAKES ENOUGH FOR 4–6 AS AN ACCOMPANIMENT

I love this simple chutney. It's so good spooned over the lamb seekh kebabs on page 96: you will be amazed how the flavours work together. If you're serving this to guests, they'll probably be wondering what the heck went into it, it's such an interesting flavour combo.

Admittedly, the first time I tried a similar chutney, I couldn't figure it out either. I'm usually quite good at recognizing ingredients but not with this one. You can simply purchase the required smooth mango chutney or try my recipe on page 142. See photograph on page 143.

Small bunch of coriander (cilantro), leaves only
Large bunch of mint, leaves only
200ml (scant 1 cup) smooth mango chutney
1–4 fresh green chillies, to taste, finely chopped
2 garlic cloves, finely chopped
Juice of 1 lime
Salt

Finely chop the coriander (cilantro) and mint leaves and place in a blender with the remaining ingredients, adding salt to taste. Blend until smooth and use within three days.

MANGO CHUTNEY

MAKES 2 JARS

Mango chutney is easy to prepare. You can make it either sweet, or sweet and spicy – adding a teaspoon or so of chilli powder really gives this chutney a kick. Once you have finished cooking the chutney, you can serve it chunky or blend it until smooth. I usually make both versions from one batch.

The resulting chutney is great served with papadams and kebabs. The smooth version tastes amazing stirred into Madras and jalfrezi curries at the end of cooking. Don't add the chunky version to curries as the mango pieces will become hard and rubbery.

400g (2 cups) sugar
250ml (1 cup) distilled white vinegar
4–5 green mangoes, peeled and cubed
1 onion, chopped
Large handful of raisins
5cm (2 in) ginger, peeled and finely chopped
3 garlic cloves, finely chopped
1 tsp black mustard seeds
1 tsp chilli powder (optional)
Salt (optional)

Put the sugar and vinegar in a large saucepan and bring to a boil, stirring continuously until the sugar dissolves. Add the remaining ingredients and simmer for about 1 hour, stirring regularly until syrupy.

When it is sticky and thick to your liking you can either leave it as it is or blend until smooth (or blend half, see introduction). Transfer to hot sterilized jars (see page 139), leaving a little space at the top.

Clockwise, from top left: red onion chutney; kashmiri red chilli and garlic chutney; mint, coriander and mango chutney; tamarind chutney.

TAMARIND CHUTNEY

MAKES 2 JARS

Tamarind chutney simply has to be on the table when my wife and I plan a curry party. It's sweet, sour, savoury and spicy, and also has a nice crunch to it. What more could you ask for in a chutney?

1–2 tbsp tamarind concentrate
2 tbsp water
3 tbsp sugar
4 tbsp tomato ketchup
Juice of 1 lemon
3 fresh green chillies, finely chopped
½ onion, finely chopped
3 spring onions (scallions), finely chopped
4 tbsp finely chopped coriander (cilantro)
1 large carrot, grated
1 tsp Madras curry powder (see p16)
Salt to taste

Put all the ingredients, with salt to taste, into a small bowl and mix well. Refrigerate for at least 1 hour before serving.

CUCUMBER RAITA

MAKES 550ML (2¼ CUPS)

Delicious spooned over biryanis and kebabs. If you want to make it even more exciting, try adding a few small chunks of cooked potato and/or finely chopped green chilli.

420g (2 cups) Greek yoghurt
3 garlic cloves, finely chopped
½ English cucumber, grated
Juice of 1 or 2 limes
Pinch each of salt and freshly ground pepper

Put all the ingredients into a bowl and whisk them together with a fork. Place in the fridge for about an hour before serving.

CHICKPEA, CARROT AND GARLIC PICKLE

THIS MAKES ENOUGH FOR 4–6 PEOPLE AS AN ACCOMPANIMENT. YOU CAN EASILY DOUBLE OR TRIPLE THE RECIPE

This one is so unique and tasty, you'll have your friends begging for the recipe. I make it all the time when I entertain and there is never any left over. It's great on papadams, naans or simply on its own.

Hats off to Eshan 'Mo' Miah, who now runs Zaman's in Newquay. Mo has never let me down with his recipes, and this one is proof of just how good his recipes can be. Please read my notes about mustard oil on page 155 before using.

1½ tsp citric acid powder (see note)
1 tbsp panch poran (see p16)
½ tsp ground turmeric
½ tsp chilli powder
Pinch of salt
20 garlic cloves, peeled
2 carrots, finely diced
6 bird's-eye green chillies
1 x 400g tin (1½ cups) chickpeas, drained
100ml (scant ½ cup) mustard oil
2 Indian bay leaves (cassia leaves)

Place all of the ingredients except the mustard oil and bay leaves in a glass bowl. Stir it all up and place in the fridge to marinate for 24 hours.

The next day, heat the mustard oil in a saucepan. When visibly hot, add the bay leaves and the marinated vegetables. Cook for 3–5 minutes and no longer. Set aside to cool completely before eating, although I have to admit I find it hard to wait for this pickle to cool before I start snacking.

NOTE: Citric acid powder is used in commercially available curry pastes and pickles. You could substitute amchoor (dried mango powder) if you want a natural alternative, but it isn't as strong. Citric acid is available from Asian grocers and in chemist shops.

TAKEAWAY-STYLE PAKORA SAUCE

MAKES ABOUT 300ML (1¼ CUPS)

If it's Indian takeaway-style pakora sauce you like, this is a good one. Usually this sweet-and-sour sauce is red from food colouring, and does look the part when bright red. The mango chutney and ketchup are already quite sweet but you might want to add a little sugar. The sour flavours come from the lemon and mint sauce. Just try it and adjust until you are happy with the flavour.

1 onion, finely chopped
2 tbsp smooth mango chutney
3 tbsp tomato ketchup
1 tsp mint sauce
200g (scant 1 cup) plain yoghurt
½ tsp roasted cumin seeds (see p12)
½ tsp chilli powder, or to taste
1 tbsp sugar
Lemon juice, to taste
½ tsp red food colouring powder (optional)
Milk (optional)
Salt

Whisk all the ingredients together, except for the food colouring, milk and salt. Once the sauce is nicely combined, check for seasoning and add salt to taste. Add food colouring, if using. If the sauce is too thick, stir in a little milk until you are happy with the consistency.

CORIANDER, GARLIC AND CHILLI RAITA

MAKES 500–550ML (2 CUPS)

My favourite raita. Nothing more to be said.

Bunch of fresh coriander (cilantro), leaves only
1–2 garlic cloves, to taste
2 tbsp lime juice
2 fresh green chillies, or to taste, roughly chopped
375g (1¾ cups) plain yoghurt
Salt

In a spice grinder or small food processor, blend the coriander (cilantro) leaves, garlic, lime juice and chillies to a paste. You can also use a pestle and mortar to do this, with a little more work.

Whisk the yoghurt with a fork until creamy smooth then stir in the coriander paste. Season with salt to taste and chill in the fridge for about 30 minutes before serving.

TOMATO, ONION AND CHILLI CHUTNEY

THIS MAKES ENOUGH FOR 4–6 PEOPLE AS AN ACCOMPANIMENT. YOU CAN EASILY DOUBLE OR TRIPLE THE RECIPE

This quick and easy chutney goes well with pretty much everything. With such bright flavours and colours, it should never be left off your curry feast table.

5 tomatoes, deseeded and finely chopped
1 onion, finely chopped
2–3 green chillies, to taste, finely chopped
3 tbsp finely chopped fresh coriander (cilantro)
Salt

Mix the tomatoes, onion, chillies and coriander (cilantro) in a bowl and add salt to taste. Place in the fridge for the flavours to develop for about an hour. Serve as a topping on whatever dish you want.

HONEY MUSTARD RAITA

MAKES JUST OVER 250ML (1 CUP)

This is a delicious dip for papadams, kebabs, samosas and chicken pakora. I love to serve it with crab samosas (see page 39).

210g (1 cup) plain yoghurt
3 tbsp finely chopped coriander (cilantro)
1 tbsp honey
Juice of 1 lime
2 tbsp rapeseed oil
1 tbsp mustard seeds
10 fresh curry leaves (optional, but don't use dried)
½ tsp ground turmeric
1 tbsp garlic and ginger paste (see p18)
Salt

Put the yogurt, coriander (cilantro), honey and lime juice in a bowl and whisk until smooth and creamy. Set aside. Heat the oil in a small frying pan over a high heat and add the mustard seeds. When they begin to pop, reduce the heat and add the curry leaves, turmeric and garlic and ginger paste. Stir for about 30 seconds. Pour the hot oil over the yoghurt mixture and whisk briskly again to prevent the yoghurt from curdling. Check for seasoning and sprinkle with salt to taste.

MINT CHUTNEY

MAKES ENOUGH FOR 4–6 AS AN ACCOMPANIMENT

This is probably the most popular chutney served in Indian restaurants. Some chefs add a little food colouring to make it bright green.

270g (1¼ cups) plain yoghurt
1 tbsp garlic and ginger paste (see p18)
1–3 bird's-eye green chillies, to taste, very finely chopped
Juice of 1 lime
1–2 tbsp commercial mint sauce of your choice, to taste
Pinch of salt

Place the ingredients in a mixing bowl and whisk to combine until smooth. Cover and place in the fridge for at least 30 minutes, before serving.

You don't need a tandoor oven to make great-tasting, fluffy naans. Sure, it's nice to use a tandoor, and I often do, but this pan method is much easier and worth a try. I guarantee you that the naans you make at home on your hob will be just as good as most takeaways, if not better.

NAANS
MAKES ENOUGH TO SERVE 8–10

900g (7 cups) plain white flour, plus extra for dusting
Scant 1 tbsp salt
2 tbsp baking powder
300ml (1¼ cups) full-fat milk
1 x 7g sachet (2½ tsp) dried yeast
2 tbsp sugar
3 eggs
270g (1¼ cups) Greek yoghurt
Oil, for greasing
3 tbsp melted ghee
Nigella seeds (black onion seeds), to sprinkle

Sift the flour, salt and baking powder into a large bowl. Heat the milk in the microwave or on the hob until hand hot. Pour into a jug (if heated on the hob), add the yeast and sugar, and whisk it all together. Cover with a cloth and leave in a warm place for about 20 minutes. It should foam right up. If it doesn't, don't worry, your naans will still rise.

Lightly beat the eggs and yoghurt together. Pour the yeasty milk mixture into the flour, along with the whisked eggs and yoghurt, and mix everything to combine.

Tip the dough out onto a work surface and knead for about 10 minutes until you have a soft, slightly sticky dough ball. Brush the insides of the bowl with a little oil and place the dough back in the bowl. Cover and allow to rise for at least 1 hour or up to 24 hours. Longer rising times achieve a tasty sourdough.

Pull a chunk of dough, about the size of a tennis ball, from the risen dough. Using your hands or a rolling pin, roll the ball out on a lightly floured work surface into a flat, circular disc or teardrop shape, about 5mm (¼ in) thick. Slap the disc between your hands to get all the excess flour off.

Heat a dry frying pan over a high heat and, when very hot, place the naan in it. It will begin to cook on the underside then bubble on the top. Check the bottom regularly to ensure it doesn't burn. If it begins to get too dark, turn the naan over to get a bit of colour on the other side. Each naan should take no more than 3–5 minutes to cook.

Remove the cooked naan to a plate, brush with a little ghee and sprinkle with nigella seeds. Keep warm while you cook the remaining dough in the same way.

OPTIONAL EXTRA: This recipe is for fluffy lightly browned naans. If you prefer a more charred appearance, place the finished naans under a hot grill (broiler) for about a minute or to your liking.

Peshawari naans take some experimentation to get right. I don't really have a sweet tooth, so if they're too sweet, I just don't like them. That is of course not the case with many people, who love them very sweet.

Therefore, please use this recipe as a guide. Feel free to adjust it to your own tastes when making the paste. With a bit of practice, you will find a recipe that is exactly as you want your Peshawari naans to be.

If you have any leftover dough, it can be kept in the fridge for up to 3 days, or frozen. If you're planning a curry evening with friends, why not make a selection of naans? Place a plate each of plain, keema and Peshawari naans on the table and you'll be everyone's best friend.

PESHAWARI NAANS
MAKES ENOUGH TO SERVE 8–10

1 quantity naan dough
    (see p146), ready to shape
Flour, for dusting
3 tbsp melted ghee
Sesame seeds, to sprinkle

FOR THE PESHAWARI PASTE
200g (2½ cups) almond flakes
2 tbsp desiccated coconut
3 tbsp single (light) cream
1 tbsp sugar, or to taste
20 sultanas (golden raisins)

First make the paste. In a food processor, blend the almond flakes, coconut, cream, sugar and sultanas (golden raisins) until they form a thick paste. You may need to add more cream if it is too crumbly, or more almond flakes if too wet. Remove from the processor and knead into a pliable dough-like paste.

Pull off a ball of naan dough the size of a tennis ball, flatten slightly and place a piece of Peshawari slightly larger than a golf ball in the middle of the dough.

Fold the naan dough around the paste and roll out following the method on page 146 for plain naan. Cook in a hot, dry frying pan in the same way, then brush with ghee and sprinkle with sesame seeds to finish.

Keep warm while you cook the rest of the naans.

I've found that keema naans are best cooked in a tandoor or very hot oven on a pizza stone. They are difficult to get right in a frying pan because of the meat inside.

The trick is to roll them out while keeping the meat inside. With a little practice, you'll roll out your naans and the minced meat inside will be thin and flavourful just like at the best restaurants.

I often substitute homemade tandoori masala for the mixed powder in the lamb mince. I like both versions, so you might like to give both a try.

KEEMA NAANS
MAKES ENOUGH TO SERVE 8–10

1 quantity naan dough
  (see p146), ready to shape
Flour, for dusting
Melted ghee, for brushing
Fresh coriander (cilantro),
  to finish

FOR THE KEEMA
400g (14 oz) lamb mince
½ onion, finely chopped
2 green chillies, finely chopped
  or mashed into a paste
2 tbsp mixed powder (see p17)
1 tsp garlic and ginger paste
  (see p18)
Pinch each of salt and freshly
  ground pepper

Preheat the oven to its highest setting and place a pizza stone on a rack to heat for about 1 hour.

Meanwhile, combine all the keema ingredients in a large mixing bowl. Knead the meat for about 5 minutes, scraping the meat against the bottom of the bowl as you do so. You want to see streaks of minced meat clinging to the surface.

Pull off a piece of naan dough the size of a tennis ball and roll out on a floured surface to about 3mm thick. Place a ball of minced meat, slightly larger than a golf ball, in the middle of the disc and wrap the dough around it.

Lightly roll out the filled disc, flipping it over a couple of times as you do. Be careful not to press too hard while rolling, or the meat will become exposed. If this happens, patch the area with a small piece of dough.

Brush the shaped naan with just a little melted ghee and place on the heated pizza stone in the oven. Bake for about 3 minutes, then flip it over and cook for another 3 minutes. Check the dough and filling are done, and cook for longer if needed.

To serve, sprinkle with coriander (cilantro) and perhaps a little more melted ghee. Keep warm while you roll and bake the remaining naans.

TIP: If you don't have a pizza stone, you can use a baking tray, although it will not get as hot.

You know those chapatis available at the supermarket? Well, don't bother. Make your own and you will be much happier. These are so much fluffier and worth every minute you spend making them.

It's important to slap them around in your hands a few times before adding them to the pan. This helps get rid of any excess flour that will burn when dry-fried. These are great served with curries or wrapped around kebabs. All you really need though, is a little butter and you'll be in chapati heaven.

You can make delicious chapatis in a pan, but if you have a gas burner, use it. You can throw them directly onto the flame, which gives them more character and makes them lighter.

CHAPATIS
MAKES 8–10 SMALL CHAPATIS

250g (2 cups) chapati flour, plus extra for dusting
About 125ml (½ cup) water
Rapeseed oil, for oiling the pan

Put the flour into a bowl and add the water a little at a time. Knead until you have a soft, pliable dough, then continue kneading for about 3 minutes. Dust the work surface with a little flour and divide the dough into 8–10 balls.

Working in batches, depending on space in your kitchen (keep the waiting balls covered with a damp tea towel), flatten each ball between your hands and then flatten them more with a rolling pin until they are about 12cm (4½ in) in diameter and 1mm thick. Dust off any excess flour from a disc of dough then slap it from hand to hand to remove any stubborn flour.

Oil the pan with just enough oil to create a film (½ tsp should do) and dry-fry the chapati for 30 seconds, then flip it over and fry for another 30 seconds. Brown spots should appear on both sides. If you are cooking on an electric hob, turn the chapati over again and apply pressure to the surface with a spatula or kitchen towel. It should puff up with air. If it doesn't it should still be fine.

If you are cooking over a gas flame, lift the chapati out of the pan and carefully place it directly on the flame. This will cause it to puff up into a nice light chapati.

Transfer to a bowl lined with kitchen paper to keep warm while you make the remaining chapatis. For best results, serve immediately, but they can also be warmed up in the microwave if necessary.

BASMATI RICE RECIPES

PREPARATION FOR STEAMED AND BOILED METHODS

The rice recipes here all serve 4. It's important not to keep rice warm for over an hour, and always reheat cooked rice fully before use.

Plan on 185g (1 cup) basmati rice for every 2 people.

Put the uncooked rice in a large bowl and cover with cold water. Swirl the water around with your hands; it will become milky from the rice starch. Pour the water out and add fresh water and repeat until the water is almost clear. About five times should do the job.

Leave the rice to soak in the last batch of fresh water for about 30 minutes. Drain and then follow any of the following recipes.

STEAMED RICE

Never fill your pan more than one-third full or the rice will not cook correctly. If making a larger batch, remember the uncooked rice-to-water volume (not weight) ratio is always 1 measure of rice to 1½ water.

370g (2 cups) basmati rice
750ml (3 cups) cold water
Pinch of salt
1 tbsp ghee or butter

Rinse and soak the rice as above, then drain. Place the rice, water, salt and ghee or butter in a saucepan. Cover with a tight-fitting lid and bring to a boil over a high heat. As soon as the water boils, remove from the heat and let it sit, lid on, for 40 minutes. Don't remove the lid. After 40 minutes, your rice will be perfectly done. Using a fork or chopstick, separate the rice grains, stirring very slowly. Basmati rice has a tendency to turn to mush if stirred too vigorously.

BOILED RICE

You can cook a lot more rice using this method, and the water-to-rice ratio isn't as important. You need to cook with enough water so that the grains of rice can float around freely as it simmers. This is my preferred method when I am preparing rice for a fried rice recipe.

750ml (3 cups) cold water
370g (2 cups) basmati rice
Pinch of salt
A little butter

Rinse and soak the rice as opposite, then drain.

Bring a large saucepan of the water to a boil then add the rice. Stir in the salt and butter, reduce the heat and simmer for about 7–9 minutes. To check for doneness, take out a couple of grains and press them with your fingers. They should be soft but still have a bit of resistance to them.

Carefully pour the rice into a colander. If serving immediately, transfer to a serving dish and your job is done. If storing for later, rinse with cold water, carefully stir through and place in an airtight container in the fridge for up to 4 days.

COLOURED RICE

A cookbook of curry-house recipes wouldn't be complete if I didn't explain how to make coloured rice. You probably already know it's done with food colouring, but if you don't, it is. Powdered food colouring is normally used when the rice is still moist from cooking. You can use the colours of your choice. Here is one option.

Place your cooked rice on a large plate and mentally divide it into quarters. Stir red food colouring powder into one quarter, green into another, and leave the rest white. Let it stand for a few minutes and then mix it all up again.

PILAU RICE

SERVES 4

Pilau rice is one of those dishes I insist on cooking with ghee. I also prefer to steam it, as the flavour of the spices infuses better with the rice. If you are cooking for a large group, you might be better off frying cold cooked basmati rice, as in the fried rice recipe below.

370g (2 cups) basmati rice
3 tbsp milk
Pinch of saffron threads
3 tbsp ghee
6 green cardamom pods, lightly bruised
5cm (2in) piece of cinnamon stick or cassia bark
1 tsp cumin seeds
1 onion, finely chopped
1 garlic clove, smashed
750ml (3 cups) cold water or unsalted chicken stock
2 Indian bay leaves (cassia leaves)
Salt

Rinse and soak the rice following the method on page 151. While it is soaking, heat the milk in a small pan until it begins to simmer. Take off the heat and stir in the saffron. Leave to infuse for about 15 minutes.

Meanwhile, melt the ghee over a medium high-heat in a saucepan that has a tight-fitting lid. When good and hot and beginning give off a nutty aroma, toss in the whole spices and cook for about 30 seconds until they become fragrant. Add the onion and sizzle for about 5 minutes until it is translucent and soft.

Add the garlic to the pan, followed by the drained rice. Stir this all up so that the rice is evenly coated in the ghee. Pour in the water or stock, add the bay leaves, then cover the pan. When the rice begins to boil and the water foams, remove from the heat and let it sit, covered and undisturbed for 40 minutes.

After 40 minutes, lift the lid and pour the saffron milk mixture over the top. Carefully stir through the rice using a fork or chopstick, until the grains of rice are nice and fluffy. Don't stir too vigorously as basmati rice has a tendency to split. Season with salt to taste and transfer to a warm bowl to serve.

FRIED RICE

SERVES 2 OR MORE AS PART OF A MULTI-COURSE MEAL

You can get really creative with fried rice. For onion fried rice, simply fry some onion in the oil and then stir in your cold, cooked rice. You could also make a fried rice version of the pilau rice above using this method. The following lemon rice recipe is the perfect accompaniment for fish curries.

3 tbsp rapeseed oil or ghee
1 tsp garlic and ginger paste (see p18)
Finely grated zest of 2 lemons and juice of 1 or 2
500ml (2 cups) cold cooked basmati rice (see p151)
3 chives, finely chopped
Salt

Heat the oil or ghee in a large frying pan over a medium-high heat until bubbling hot. Add the garlic and ginger paste and lemon zest, and fry for about 30 seconds. Add the cold rice and stir gently for about 2 minutes until all the rice grains are nicely coated with the oil. When the rice is really hot, squeeze in the lemon juice. Season with salt to taste and top with the chopped chives to serve.

LIST OF INGREDIENTS

Ajwain (carom) seeds
Ajwain seeds are not actually seeds but small fruit. They smell a lot like thyme but their flavour is more of a cross between fennel seeds and oregano, but much stronger. They have a pungent, bitter flavour and should be used sparingly as they can easily overpower a dish.

Amchoor (dried mango powder)
Amchoor powder, made from dried and ground mango, has a strong citric flavour and is really good added to tandoori masalas or any curry that benefits from a citric kick.

Asafoetida
In its raw powder form, asafoetida smells terrible. Once fried, its aroma and flavour are much more pleasing, like fried onions. This spice is used sparingly as it is quite strong. Its most common use in BIR cooking is to be tempered in oil with other ingredients to make a tarka for dishes such as tarka dhal.

Basmati rice
The rice you serve with the recipes in this book has got to be basmati. It has a nutty flavour all its own. Basmati benefits from ageing so look for the longest grain, aged basmati rice you can find. It's a little more expensive but worth every penny. Both Tilda and East End Foods supply top quality basmati rice.

Bay leaves (Indian, Western)
Indian bay leaves come from the cassia tree and taste like cassia and cinnamon. They are available from Asian grocers and some larger supermarkets. Western bay leaves are what you probably already use in your spaghetti Bolognese and meat stews. I don't think any more explanation is necessary.

Black salt
This fine salt has the disadvantage of smelling like eggs gone off, due to its high sulphur content. Don't be put off by the smell, though. It is a key ingredient for homemade chaat masala and also tastes fantastic sprinkled sparingly over a host of other dishes. There is no substitute, so if a recipe calls for it, do your best to source it. It's available from Asian grocers and online.

Cardamom (black and green)
By weight, cardamom is the third most expensive spice in the world, beaten to the top spots only by vanilla and saffron. Green cardamom is most often used in BIR cooking, added to garam masalas and tempered whole in oil. The seeds are what impart the flavour, so the pods are often lightly crushed before adding to get that flavour into the dish. Black cardamom are bigger and have a significantly stronger, smoky flavour. If you need to substitute one type for the other, use half as many black as green.

Cassia bark *See cinnamon*

Chillies (fresh)
Fresh chillies range in heat from quite mild to numbingly spicy. I usually use green bird's-eye and bullet chillies for the recipes in this book. That said, I do like to experiment with other chillies as they all have their own unique flavour in addition to their heat level. Fresh chillies can be used simply split down the middle, finely or roughly chopped, or blended into a chilli paste, as my recipes demonstrate.

Chilli Powder
The preferred chilli powder at most curry houses is Kashmiri chilli powder. It is quite spicy and has a nice flavour too. Kashmiri chilli powder is available at Asian grocers and also some supermarkets. How spicy your curries are is really a personal thing. I use Kashmiri chilli powder in my cooking but you might like to experiment with milder or hotter chilli powders.

Cinnamon
Almost all of the cinnamon powder sold around the world is actually made from cassia bark. More often than not, the labelling is not deceptive, with cassia labelled 'cinnamon cassia'. Powdered cassia can be used in both savoury and sweet recipes for a nice, warming kick, and tastes almost identical to real cinnamon powder. Although it tastes great, there is a lot of new medical evidence that has demonstrated that cassia in regular doses can cause liver damage. I don't feel there is much to worry about if you only cook with it from time to time but then I'm not a medical expert. If you use whole or ground cinnamon regularly, use Ceylon or 'true cinnamon'. It costs a little more and it's what I use.

If you are looking for 'true cinnamon', it will usually be stated on the label. If in doubt, 'true cinnamon' is only grown in Sri Lanka, the Seychelles and Madagascar. Cassia bark comes from China and Indonesia.

Cloves
These offer a sweet, recognizable flavor that is excellent in spice masalas and for tempering in oil. Cloves have a low smoking point so they can burn faster than most spices and need to be watched if roasting.

Coconut milk, flour and block
Coconut flour and block coconut are most often used in BIR curries, whereas coconut milk is more popular in authentic Indian curries. You can substitute one for the other but when using coconut milk, you might need to reduce the sauce down more.

Cumin
White cumin seeds have a strong flavour and aroma and are hugely popular in Indian and other cooking. Cumin is in fact the second most popular spice in the world, second

only to black pepper. The seeds can be tempered whole and are also nice added in ground form to many dishes.

Black cumin seeds (royal cumin) are darker and thinner than the white seeds. They are sweeter and nuttier than white and also stronger in flavour, so used sparingly. They add a nice touch to special dishes.

Curry leaves
My favourite ingredient of all time, these small leaves smell amazing when tempered in a little oil. They are used a lot more in southern Indian cooking but many British curry-house chefs have started adding them to their northern Indian, Pakistani and Bangladeshi dishes too. Use fresh or frozen leaves as dried curry leaves have a much weaker flavour.

Fennel seeds
Fennel seeds have a nice flavour, similar to black liquorice and star anise. Star anise is slightly stronger but I do use the two spices together and also substitute the whole spices for each other if I've run out of one. Fennel seeds can be tempered whole in oil and also added later to a sauce as a ground spice.

Fenugreek (methi)
You can purchase fenugreek as a powder, whole seeds or as dried leaves. The dried leaves are used most in British Indian cookery.

Ghee
This is clarified butter but it doesn't taste like homemade clarified butter. They must feed the cows something different over there in India. It is available from Asian grocers, and many supermarkets now stock it. Ghee doesn't need to be refrigerated and should last, covered, for months. There was a time when curry-house curries were sodden in the stuff. Nowadays, healthier alternatives are being used, like cold-pressed rapeseed oil, but ghee is still hugely popular and a great way of getting a nice buttery flavour into your dishes.

Mace See nutmeg

Mustard oil
There's no substitute for mustard oil and I love the stuff. It has a pungent and strong flavour and has been used for centuries in northern Indian and Bangladeshi cooking. It is available in the UK and US but has not been approved for human consumption. If you decide to go for it and break the rules, be sure to heat it up until it smokes and then let it cool before heating up again to use in your cooking.

Mustard seeds (black)
Mustard seeds are available as black or yellow, but I use the black variety in the recipes in this book, which need to be tempered in very hot oil. Once they start popping, the heat can be reduced and their pungent flavour will be released into the oil. Mustard seeds require this high heat but most whole spices don't. Once the mustard seeds have begun popping in the oil, other whole spices with lower smoking points can be added.

Nigella seeds (black onion seeds)
Although nigella seeds are often called black onion seeds, they aren't actually from the onion family. Whatever you call them, they are excellent sprinkled over homemade naans.

Nutmeg and mace
Like most spices, nutmeg is best purchased whole and then ground as, once ground, it loses its flavour quickly. The small, hard round nutmeg is the seed of the nutmeg tree and is harvested from the inside of the nutmeg fruit. Crack one of the fruit open and you'll find a red, lacy covering around the seed. This is mace. Both mace and nutmeg are similar in flavour but nutmeg is a lot stronger than the more delicate mace, and should be added to curries only in small doses. The dried mace is nice tempered in oil and is often used ground with cardamom seeds to make cardamom and mace powder.

Paneer
This is the most simple of cheeses. Indian paneer is now widely available in Asian shops and in supermarkets.

For the recipes in this book, commercially bought paneer will do fine.

Rose water
Rose water is made by steeping rose petals in water, and is cheap, so there's no need to go out picking rose petals. This fragrant water is added to rice, biryanis, kormas and other dishes to make them taste and smell even better.

Saffron
By weight, saffron is the most expensive spice on the planet, worth more than gold. Luckily, you don't need a lot, as a little goes a long way. Saffron consists of the stigma of the crocus flower. Only three stigma grow on each flower, which have to be picked by hand. That's why it's so expensive. Many restaurants use turmeric instead of saffron to give their food colour. I use saffron threads in my recipes, which add a much better flavour than powdered.

Star Anise See fennel seeds.

Tamarind
Tamarind is available both in block form and as a concentrated paste. Tamarind concentrate will work just fine in my recipes and it's a lot less work. It has a strong acidic flavour like a strong vinegar.

Turmeric
Turmeric is one of the spices that make Indian food what it is. It has a distinctive woody, bitter flavour that is popular in curries and rice. It is often used as a substitute for saffron, for its colour, though it tastes nothing like it. Its deep yellow colour gives food an appetizing appearance, and as it is quite bitter, it is used sparingly.

Yoghurt (Greek, plain)
Full-fat Greek yoghurt is perfect for marinating meat, poultry, seafood, paneer and vegetables. I also prepare thick raitas with it. For thinner raitas and for use in sauces, use plain natural yoghurt, which doesn't curdle as easily.

ONLINE INGREDIENT SOURCES

MEAT, SEAFOOD AND VEGETABLE SOURCES

Farmer's Choice
Specializing in free-range meat, Farmer's Choice work with respected British free-range farmers. They also supply sustainably caught seafood and organically grown vegetables, delivered to your doorstep. www.farmerschoice.co.uk

Alternative Meats
If you're looking for something a little different, try Alternative Meats. Where possible, they offer British-reared meat such as Wagyu beef, goat, mutton, buffalo, suckling pig and wild boar. If you want to try something a little more exotic, they also offer an impressive range of hard-to-find meat like crocodile, springbok, kangaroo, ostrich, venison and zebra. www.alternativemeats.co.uk

Delishfish
An excellent online source for fresh and exotic seafood. Check out their catch of the day for cod, haddock and halibut that is caught off the northeast Scottish coast. They also supply a fantastic range of other seafood that tastes great in a curry or on the barbecue. www.delishfish.co.uk

ONLINE SPICE SOURCES (UK)

East End Foods
A sponsor of my blog, I have visited the East End Foods production facilities and I can trust them to deliver excellent quality spices and basmati rice. I buy the whole spices to roast and grind into my own masala blends, but they also supply good quality garam masala, curry powder and other pre-ground spices. East End Foods' spices and basmati rice are available at supermarkets and Asian grocers. They also have a brilliant online shop. www.store.eastendfoods.co.uk

Absolute Spice
I have been very impressed with the top-quality spices that Absolute Spice supply. They deliver to over 30 countries. www.absolutespice.com

Spices of India
You will love this site. In addition to groceries and spices, you will also find a fantastic range of kitchen and tableware. www.spicesofindia.co.uk

Nisbets
Suppliers of cookware. www.nisbets.co.uk/homechef

Dr. Burnörium's Extraordinary Hot Sauce Emporium
Want to add a lot more heat to your curries? Check out this site. You'll find everything from the hottest naga chilli powders to mind-blowing sauces and pickles. www.hotsauceemporium.co.uk

A bit of fun
I can highly recommend the Indian food tour by Secret Food Tours in London. You will visit the famous Lahore Kebab House in Shoreditch and Eastern Eye in Brick Lane among many other places of interest. www.secretfoodtours.com

ONLINE SPICE SOURCES (US)

The Savory Spice Shop
Large range of spices. www.savoryspiceshop.com

Penzeys
Another large range of spices. www.penzeys.com

iShopIndian.com
Groceries and utensils. www.ishopindian.com

Ancient Cookware
A large range of cookware from India and around the world. www.ancientcookware.com

Mohini
A small but excellent supplier of top quality Indian spice blends in my hometown of Turlock, California. www.mohinisblends.com

INDEX